THE SHRINE OF THE BLACK MADONNA AND THE AFROCENTRIC PERSONALITY

A DISSERTATION
SUBMITTED TO THE FACULTY OF CLARK ATLANTA UNIVERSITY
IN PARTIAL FULFILLMENT OF THE REQUIREMENTS FOR
THE DEGREE OF DOCTOR OF ARTS IN HUMANITIES

BY

LEON DAVIS

AFRICAN-AMERICAN STUDIES/AFRICANA WOMEN'S STUDIES, AND
HISTORY

ATLANTA, GEORGIA

authorHOUSE

AuthorHouse™
1663 Liberty Drive
Bloomington, IN 47403
www.authorhouse.com
Phone: 833-262-8899

Published by AuthorHouse 11/25/2020

ISBN: 978-1-6655-0862-9 (sc)
ISBN: 978-1-6655-0861-2 (e)

ACKNOWLEDGMENTS

My sincere gratitude goes to all of the people who gave me the materials and direction needed for the creation of this dissertation. The faculty, who gave me the encouragement and direction I needed, the people of the Shrine of the Black Madonna, and the help of people in Woodruff Library were essential in my endeavor. Dr. Josephine Bradley was instrumental in my final choice of a research topic. I would like to thank Deborah Jones Arnold and Ms. Jacqui Jackson for their assistance. I also thank Dr. Joseph A. Baldwin for his great contribution of the Afrocentric Personality Test and his interest in this project. I would also like to thank Dr. Thomas Scott and Dr. K. B. S. Barrow for helpful comments and advice.

TABLE OF CONTENTS

LIST OF FIGURES

LIST OF TABLES

ABBREVIATIONS

ASC   African self-consciousness

ASEO   African

AWO   African world order

BCN   Black Christian nationalist

CEO   Chief Executive Officer

KUA   Small group

MSTA   Morrish Science Temple Association

NAACP   National Association for the Advancement of Colored People

NCLC   Northern Christian Leadership Conference

NOI   Nation of Islam

PAOCC   Pan African Orthodox Christian Church

U.N.I.A.   United Negro Improvement Association

CHAPTER I

INTRODUCTION

The purpose of this study was to investigate whether or not the Shrine of the Black Madonna engenders an Afrocentric personality in its members. This research focuses on analyzing the phenomenon of an Afrocentric personality from a practical perspective rather than a theoretical one. This analysis, therefore, utilizes the practical approach as it relates to the Shrine of the Black Madonna in the effort of nation building and maintenance. The Shrine of the Black Madonna emphasizes the African culture within the organization.

If someone is grounded in an African way of life, then that person will have an Afrocentric worldview, exhibit an Afrocentric personality and is a person who has adopted African cultures and traditions. This also indicates that an African worldview will personify African morals and values as an important center of reference. The Afrocentric worldview uses African people as its subject. It reflects an African lifestyle. The African economic model is the center of the person's ideology on living peaceably. The person has communal living arrangements and communal dinners. The Shrine has a communal farm called the Beulah Land Farm.

The existence of communal socialization as practiced by members of the Shrine of the Black Madonna has resulted in members who may be described as having an Afrocentric personality. An African personality is the African-American view of a

1

holistic personality. The ideal healthy person is grounded in the African ideology of Sudicism. Sudicism (when one is in touch with nature) is the spiritual commitment to an ideological view of harmony. Even in the construct of this type of organization, the person must be in harmony with the group, because an undisciplined person creates disharmony within the organization. It is the quest for harmony that is at the source of all literary, rhetorical, or behavioral actions; the Sudic ideal, which emphasizes the primacy of a person, can only function if the person seeks individual and collective harmony.[1] There are two scholars who advocate African centered psychology. Joseph Baldwin uses self-consciousness as a model for an Afrocentric personality and Na'im Akbar dscribes the African personality as composed of the soul, mind, Ba, social, and tribal selves. The Kemetians describe two other facets to this personality: the Ka, or shadow, and Seb, the reproductive soul.

Albert Cleage was the founding father of the Shrine of the Black Madonna, an organization that has a nationalistic philosophy and emphasizes African culture. The adoption and internalization of African philosophies tend to produce a specific worldview. The culture of a people is reflected in their language, child rearing practices, naming, and institutions, which produce a specific personality; thus the African personality will have an African world view. For example, a person's culture or ethnicity can be revealed by his or her name. The Shrine encourages an Afrocentric ethos emphasizing the use of African names for its members.

---

[1] Molefi Kete Asante, *The Afrocentric Idea* (Philadelphia: Temple University Press, 1987), 185.

The Shrine of the Black Madonna conducts workshops and a training series to educate its members about the culture of Africa. For example, members learn African languages, including Swahili and Yoruba. John Henrik Clark and many Continental Africans emphasize the importance of language. John Henrik Clark states that when Europeans colonized the world, they colonized information about the world. Also, in his book, *Decolonizing the Mind,* Ngugi wa Thiong'o, the Kenyan critic and novelist, has argued that the imposition of the European language on Africans furthers the oppression of the people because their chances for mental liberation become remote. The intended result of this mental colonization is despair, despondency, and a collective death wish.[2]

Through the indoctrination rituals of the Shrine of the Black Madonna, new members become a part of their organization. The aspiration of this nationalist organization is to create an African nation that is composed of Afrocentric personalities. These rituals are tools used to convert individuals from Negroes to blacks or Africans. The conversion experience can be identified by the member's level of Afrocentricity through their behavior.[3]

Rationale of the Study

The existence of nationalist organizations in the black community goes back to the Marcus Garvey movement of the 1920s, as well as many other groups such as the Moorish Science Temple (MSTA) founded by Noble Drew Ali and the Nation of Islam. The researcher, as a student at an Historically Black University during the 1960s, has

---

[2] Ngugi Wa Thiong'o, *Decolonizing the Mind: The Politics of Language in Africans Literature* (Chicago: Third World Press, 1993), 1.

[3] Tenth Anniversary, Shrine #10, *National Tribute to Jeramogi Abebe Agyeman,* June 1987. 106-107.

struggled to understand why the masses of blacks refuse to join and support black organizations that offer a program for black liberation that could benefit the masses of Africans in this country and the world at large. Joseph Baldwin and other scholars have written about the individual development of the Afrocentric personality. The reason for studying an organization such as the Shrine is to ascertain ways that black people can use the knowledge provided by black organizations for the liberation of black people.

While various organizations during the decades following reconstruction had their own unique approach to assisting black people, there was also limited commonality. The aim of the Universal Negro Improvement Association (U.N.I.A.) was to uplift the masses of Negroes, as they were called then, around the world. The Pan-African Orthodox Church was an institution that served the spiritual needs of the masses and similar to the U.N.I.A. stressed a renewal of Afrocentric values. The strengthening of the role of the black church was a key ingredient. The U.N.I.A. was not completely African centered culturally because of the use of Christian symbols and practice, even though they employed African symbols and dieties. The Shrine of the Black Madonna has incorporated some of the same ideological and theoretical precepts as that of the U.N.I.A. and the Pan-African Orthodox Church. The goal of the Shrine is the liberation of black people. Amos Wilson states that the theology of the Shrine of the Black Madonna in good part is borrowed from orthodox sources which have been significantly "Africanized." Therefore, this theology is uniquely its own creation, as well as being instrumental in advancing the exclusive interests of the Shrine and its black members.

However, the Shrine of the Black Madonna is not a copycat imitation of Orthodox Christian philosophy.[4]

Amos Wilson clearly understood the dynamics of Afrocentrism. Janice D. Hamlet meanwhile states: "The Nation of Islam is a full-fledged black culture, a nation within a nation."[5] The Nation has a full program that meets all the needs of its members in the following areas: economics, politics, social, military, ethnical, and cosmology. The Shrine of the Black Madonna has significantly increased the knowledge base by introducing practices, curriculum, and the rituals of African communalism. By studying the organizations that have an Afrocentric base, the contributions of African ancestors will be better appreciated and perhaps even more widely imitated.

Statement of the Problem

The African-American in American society experiences economic dependency, psychological hardship, political powerlessness, and cultural alienation. The existence of cultural alienation is the most destructive aspect of the problem that Africans in America experience. Black people have been influenced by Eurocentric cultural hegemony which is that one group can be ruled or dominated by another group.

Thus, this study of the Shrine of the Black Madonna attempts to understand how this organization cultivates Afrocentric personalities in its members. The distinction between Afrocentric and mainstream organizational theories should be noted while

---

[4] Amos N. Wilson, *Blueprint for Black Power: A Moral, Political, and Economic Imperative for the Twenty-First Century* (New York: Afrikan World Infosystems, 1998), 81.

[5] Janice D. Hamlet, ed., *Afrocentric Visions* (Thousand Oaks, CA: Sage Publications, 1998), 73.

investigating the theories and ideologies of Afrocentrism in this organization.

According to Hamlet:

> The limited conception of human identity found in the Eurocentric model is reflected in the way the client is conceived in human service organization theory. Throughout the human service organization literature, the client is usually conceived as one individual, as if she or he lives in a vacuum and is not a part of a social group.[6]

The Afrocentric model, as exemplified by the Shrine, reflects how the African idea of the person as part of a collective, and not an isolated individual, solidifies his or her existence within the group and does not alienate him or her from black society. Hamlet indicates that "Unlike the Eurocentric sociological model, the Afrocentric model conceives the individual identity as a collective."[7] Moreover, the six assumptions of the Afrocentric model are what distinguishes it from the Eurocentric organizational theory. Those assumptions are:

1. Human beings are conceived collectively.

2. Human beings are spiritual (not just material).

3. Human beings are good by nature.

4. The affective approach to knowledge is epistemologically valid.

5. Some of human behavior is non-rational.

6. The axiology of highest values lies in interpersonal relations.[8]

---

[6] Ibid., 76.

[7] Ibid., 78.

[8] Linda J. Myers, *Understanding an Afrocentric Worldview* (Dubuque, IA: Kendall/Hunt Publishing Company, 1998), 16.

Research Questions

Research Question 1: How does the Shrine of the Black Madonna create Afrocentric personalities in its members?

Research Question 2: How will members of the Shrine using communal economics, self-knowledge and an African orientation reflect the collective identity of the African saying, "I am because we are, because we are, therefore I Am."[9]

Limitations

The quantitative findings were limited because of the sample size and the size of the population. The researcher did not use the Statistical Package for the Social Sciences (SPSS) test or any other statistical test because of these two factors. The quantitative analysis was limited to tables and figures. This qualitative study was limited to interviewing ten leaders. The participant/ observation bias did not have *the necessity of a second observer to compare notes with the observer.

Theoretical Framework

The framework for this study uses an overall theory, two macro theories, and a micro theory. The Afrocentric view is based on a highly developed holistic view. Other scholars such as Asante, Oba T'Shaka, Wade Nobles, Joseph Baldwin, and Maulana Karenga have also recognized the beginning of African-centered inquiry as beginning with David Walker.

---

[9] Ibid., V.

Meanwhile, numerous African scholars and scholar activists operating under the severest sociopolitical hegemony of non-Africans have, over the last 200 years, advanced African centered approaches in their pursuit of history, science, religion, philosophy, and politics. The attempt to suppress African culture and experience has never been limited to any sphere of human activity of which centers of study across all disciplines comprises only a part. David Walker, Drusilla Dunjee Houston, George Wells Parker, Maulana Karenga, George James, Marcus Garvey, Asa Hilliard, Walter Rodney, Imari Obadelle, and many other Afrocentric have studied this phenomenon.[10]

However, Molefi Asante has set the standard of Afrocentricity in his book, *Afrocentricity*.[11] Asante has continued to propagate this idea in recent publications. Other scholars have contributed to the development of Afrocentricity and have developed theories about the Afrocentric personality. D. A. YaAzibo has refined African personality research. In the twentieth century, Frantz Fanon's "Call to Leave Europe,"[12] is an illustrative example underscoring the renewed urgency for Africans to become centered on themselves (not to become Arab, Asian, or non-African). According to YaAzibo, "Asante crystallized and formalized the African centered approach under the heading of Afrocentricity. He confidently predicted that the Afrocentric approach would take root as a formal self-sustaining conceptual framework."[13] In his book,

---

[10] Dauoi Ajani Ya Azibo, "Pitfalls and Some Ameliorative Strategies in African Personalities Research," *Journal of Black Studies* 19, No. 3 (March 1989): 306-319.

[11] Molefi Kete Asante, *Afrocentricity* (Chicago: African-American Images, Inc., 2003), 10.

[12] Frantz Fanon, *The Wretched of the Earth*, 235.

[13] Ibid., 306.

Afrocentricity, Asante clearly states his ideas on the African personality. The philosophy of the Shrine is based on these ideas.

The Afrocentric theory, advanced by Asante, conceptualizes an African worldview. Asante sees this worldview as an alternative to the European worldview. The Eurocentric worldview has been positioned as a universal perspective. European scholars have imposed an underserving worldview on Africans and people of African descent. Europeans have looked upon Africans as insignificant objects. According to the concept of Afrocentricity, Africans are the principal subjects of study, as opposed to being objectified. The African-American view of a holistic personality, which is a healthy person, is grounded in the idea of Sudicism, or the spiritual commitment to an ideology of harmony. In the African view, the person must be harmonized, because an undisciplined person creates disharmony within society. The quest for harmony is at the source of all literary, rhetorical, or behavioral actions; the Sudic ideal, which emphasizes the primacy of person, can only function if the person seeks individual and collective harmony.[14]

J. A. Baldwin has also developed a theory of Afrocentricity involving the African personality. Baldwin's main theoretical principle is the concept of an African survival thrust. The African personality that is produced by the programs of the Shrine of the Black Madonna operates on the principle of an African survival thrust. Thus, Baldwin's theory is exemplified in the personalities of the leaders of these organizations. The

---

[14] Molefi Kete Asante, *The Afrocentric Idea* (Philadelphia: Temple University Press, 1987), 4.

emphasis on self-knowledge by these organizations is reflected in their pursuit to be

aware of and create Afrocentric situations. Baldwin states:

> The present theory of the Black or African personality, while operating from
> the premise of the interrelatedness of personality, and race, departs from the
> conceptual and philosophical framework of the Western psychological
> tradition, in all other respects. Conceptually, this theory is forged within the
> framework of African psychology.[15]

African psychology takes, as its conceptual framework, the African reality, structure of

history, philosophy, and culture, and what is generally referred to as African cosmology.

Baldwin makes several assumptions in his theory of an Afrocentric personality.

His first assumption is about the nature of the universe. He assumes that the basic nature

of human experience is social. Humans live and thrive in a social universe from which

the individual derives all meaning and significance. A person's experiential reality is

therefore primarily social. This basic premise provides the framework for the other

assumptions to follow. For example, within this framework, another assumption is that

race—one's collective biogenetic composition—constitutes the individual's fundamental

social definition; it is original, concrete, and consistent, enduring from birth until death.[16]

Baldwin's assumption is indicated by the following passage:

> Theoretically then, the individual's very first social definition is of race
> biological commonality) from which derives all other social meanings and
> significance in the social universe. Another basic assumption of this theory is
> that the individual's cosmology or worldview, that is collective reality, evolves
> directly from his/her culture. These attendant processes, cosmology and culture,
> represent the collective survival thrust of the racial group to which they are

---

[15] Molefi Kete Asante, *Afrocentricity*, 21.

[16] Joseph A. Baldwin, "Notes on an Afrocentric Theory of Black Personality," *Journal of Black Psychology 5, No. 2* (August 1987): 133-148.

indigenous. As race varies, then so does cosmology, culture, survival thrust. One could say that a basic emphasis in the African reality structure is toward unity. In short, African cosmology is said to be man-nature harmony or unity, oneness of being. In the European cosmology on the other hand, so called human nature relations are separable, compartmentalized and independent.[17]

Race and environment, along with culture, produce a specific worldview. The African worldview differs from the worldview of Europeans, and one of its distinguishing characteristics is its survival thrust. According to Baldwin, certain attributes are the core of the black personality. One aspect of the African personality is the African self-extension orientation. This orientation is deep seated, innate and unconscious and is a biogenetically defined psychological phenomenon. It has been described, in part at least, as an experience felt at the deepest physical level, a total involvement in experience, and as a spiritualistic transcendence in experience. This spirituality is believed to represent the key ingredient, which allows for self-extension to occur in the African psyche. Baldwin further explains a subset of the African self-extension orientation. However, the other subset was called the "African self-consciousness component of the black personality and this is conceptualized as the conscious process of communal phenomenology. It operates with the African self-extension orientation under normal, natural conditions."[18]

One of the Afrocentric models that are to be applied to the study of the Shrine of the Black Madonna have not been researched extensively. However, the researcher relates these models to the Shrine of the Black Madonna in order to critique it as an

---

[17] Ibid.

[18] Ibid., 134.

individual group. The ideas of Jerome H. Schiele were utilized to accomplish, with groups, what other scholars have achieved in the field of psychology with individual personalities. Schiele contends that, "In addition, the application of the Afrocentric models to organizational theory will help broaden its conceptual knowledge base as a social science model. This model will contribute to the study of Afrocentric concepts and issues (Africology) and to highlight the worldview of African people in a theory."[19]

Schiele offers a philosophical foundation, presenting the African ideas on philosophy as an anthropocentric ontology. Schiele states that, "The anthropocentric ontology was a complete unity which nothing could destroy. Also, the continuity from material to spiritual is the cosmological basis of the Afrocentric viewpoint."[20]

The Eurocentric model views the individual and nature as independent. Unlike the Eurocentric model, the Afrocentric model conceives individual identity as a part of the collective. Schiele provides the tenets of the African paradigm in the following statement:

> The Afrocentric paradigm is predicated on the traditional African philosophical assumptions that emphasize the interconnectedness and interdependency of natural phenomena. From this perspective, all modalities and realties are viewed as one, and there is no demarcation between the spiritual and material, substance and form.[21]

The Afrocentric conceptual paradigm as advocated by Schiele and Myers consists of six premises:

---

[19] Jerome Schiele, "Organizational Theory from an Afrocentric Perspective," *Journal of Black Studies.21*, No. 2 (December 1990): 149-155.

[20] Ibid., 146.

[21] Ibid., 146.

1. Human beings are conceived collectively

2. Human beings are spiritual (not just material)

3. Human beings are good

4. The affective approach to knowledge is epistemologically valid

5. Much of human behavior is non-rational

6. The axiology of highest values lies in interpersonal relations

Finally, the conceptual framework of Linda J. Myers was used as another theoretical paradigm for this study. Myers proposed a feminist model of the Afrocentric paradigm for this study called the optimal model. The optimal model is composed of methods in an Afrocentric psychology. The basis of this conceptual system is predicated on the assumptions and principles serving as the foundation of the worldview of Africans. This conceptual system has been identified as a philosophical and psychological blue print toward the achievement of everlasting peace and happiness. Myers describes an evolutionary process: the world becomes one, then two, and then one again. Hamlet surmises that:

> It is striking evidence of the natural evolutionary process of one becoming two, and then two becoming again one: the pain, insecurity, guilt, fear, anxiety and destruction of the suboptimal worldview eventually forces (re-awakens) the search for an alternative worldview (making two, in order to return to the worldview (one) that honors peace, harmony, collaboration, and the good of all.[22]

---

[22] Janice D. Hamlet, Ed., *Afrocentric Visions* (Thousand Oaks, CA: Sage Publications 1998), 74.

Theory Specific to the Study

This study uses the Afrocentric model created by Kobi K. K. Kambon (a.k.a.

Joseph A. Baldwin). Baldwin, using the Afrocentric approach in studying the African

personality, states that:

> The Afrocentric approach, on the other hand, provides the only legitimate
> African culturally based conception of the African personality. The Afrocentric
> conceptual framework interprets African psychological functioning and
> behavior from the perspective of the African worldview (i.e. philosophy,
> norms, social organizations, ceremonies and practices, etc.). This approach
> then draws its conceptual framework from the distinct history, culture and
> philosophy of African people which prioritizes the affirmation of African life,
> its cultural integrity and authenticity.[23]

Kambon recognizes other models—the Naim Akbar model and the Robert William

model.[24] Kambon states that the dynamic African spirituality of communalism and

collectivism, merging into holistic synthesis is the driving energy of the African

personality. Lynda Myers, as previously stated, indicates that the African worldview is

basically predicated on the African deep spirituality. Kambon also states: "It (African

spirituality) is biogenetic (innate) and deeply rooted in the African psyche. It is the

unconscious core of psychical energy which is immutable in the inner psychical

functioning of the African personality."[25] Kambon calls this the African self-extension

orientation. It acquires consciousness through experience, and this consciousness

functions to directly maintain, preserve, and fortify itself in the fulfillment of its inherent

---

[23] K. K. Kambon, *African Black Psychology: The American Context* 1992 (Tallahassee, FL: Nubian Nation Publications, 1998), 277.

[24] Ibid., 300-302.

[25] Ibid., 307.

or genetically programmed thrust (propensity) toward African affirmation empowerment, self-determination, and preservation (the African self-consciousness).

Kambon explains that this genetically-based African spirituality is an expression of African cosmic (spiritual) wholeness or unity. The African self-extension orientation is expressed by the African self-consciousness. The cognitive-emotional and behavioral qualities are natural and indigenous to African people regardless of social environmental conditions.[26]

Kambon names four components of the African Self Consciousness (ASC) as follows:

1. Awareness/recognition of one's (collective) African identity and cultural heritage;

2. General ideological and activity priorities placed on African survival, liberation and proactive/affirmative development;

3. Specific activity priorities placed on collective self-knowledge and self-affirmative, i.e., Afrocentric values, customs, and institution building; and

4. A posture of resolute resistance defense against anti-African, anti-black forces and threats to African survival in general[27]

Kambon proposes the overriding goals of African personality development and functioning are the vigorous expression of ASC that affirms Pan-African cultural nationalism. He suggests that the overriding goals are the attainment and maintenance of an African World Order/Pan African World Nationhood.[28] This ultimate goal of African

---

[26] Ibid., 277.

[27] Ibid., 308.

[28] Ibid., 309.

personality development and functioning is to bring about and keep the Pan-African World Nationhood through African Liberation.

The organization that is the focal point of this study is approached as examples of applied Afrocentric conceptual theory. Baldwin's Afrocentric personality theory is useful when attempting to understand what type of individuals comprise, for example, the membership of the Shrine of the Black Madonna. In addition, Myers's theory of optimal worldview was used to underline the philosophical underpinning of the organization involved in this study along with the ideas of Baldwin, Asante, and other scholars.

Baldwin's ideas of race and culture were used to measure the extent to which the culture of the Shrine of the Black Madonna uses Afrocentric cosmology as its foundation. The African concept of knowing thyself is the basis of the knowledge espoused by Baldwin's theory of survival thrust. The concepts of the optimal versus suboptimal worldviews as developed by Myers are also relevant to the study of the Shrine of the Black Madonna. The Shrine follows the seven principles of Nguzo Saba (KiSwahili for "principles") as they are developed by Maulana Karenga. The seven principles are: (1) Umoja (unity); (2) Kujichagulia (self-determination); (3) Ujima (collective work and responsibility); (4) Ujamaa (cooperative economics); (5) Nia (purpose); (6) Kuumba (creativity); and (7) Imani (faith).[29] The members of the Shrine live, work, worship, and study together. Myers' concepts of oneness and the spiritual aspect of the optimal worldview are also observable in the lives of the members of the Shrine. Religion is the

---

[29] Kambon, K.K., *African Black Psychology...*, 304.

spiritual aspect that encompasses the total being in the philosophy of the Shrine's program.

The programs of the Shrine of the Black Madonna reflect the epitome of an Afrocentric organization. Jerome Schiele's Afrocentric model encompasses the idea of the individual's existence as only a part of the group. The idea of a collective welfare is stressed by organizations that teach new members to shed the idea of personal welfare or individualism. The individual is taught that he is not only himself, but also the embodiment of his ancestors and those yet to come. This is the spiritualism that Myers identified as a component of the optimal worldview. The ideas of Schiele are valuable because the organization to be studied has Afrocentric philosophies and religious beliefs as part of the African worldview or cosmology.

Asante's concept of Afrocentricity is another viewpoint from which to study the Shrine and perhaps other organizations. The idea of being centered on the African worldview can be investigated in the programs and philosophies of the Shrine of the Black Madonna in its struggles for liberation and nationhood. This organization strives for harmony, i.e., the natural affection and loves between members of the African race, and also encourages behavior that will produce group unity and group pride or more specifically, racial pride and unity.

This study focuses on the notion that Black Nationalism in religious organizations is reflected in its members' personalities and Afrocentrism which are the basis of their organizational philosophy. The target group for this study is members of the Shrine of the Black Madonna Church which supports nationalism and Afrocentricity. The use of Asante's guidelines of being Afrocentric was also helpful in studying the people who are members of this organization. The theory of Baldwin was also useful in understanding the degree of African survival thrust that this organization possesses. It is anticipated that the African cosmology should be reflected in the communal tenets of the organization.

The Shrine of the Black Madonna is an Afrocentric organization that has an African cosmology at its center. The Shrine is considered Afrocentric because it is based on knowledge and philosophies of African people. The Shrine of the Black Madonna has a communal orientation and may be deemed holistic because it does not separate African philosophy and religion. The Baldwin theory of the Afrocentric personality was used to test organization members to determine if the ideas of Linda Myers's optimal conceptual system apply to the African worldview.

More specifically, this study was based on the theory that the Shrine of the Black Madonna is a nationalistic organization with an Afrocentric worldview. Baldwin theorized that African cosmology along with the idea of race and culture are part of the African personalities of the African race. These personalities can be measured by Baldwin's Afrocentric personality scale because membership of the Shrine of the Black Madonna is 100% black and adheres to an African cosmology and an African culture. The members were perceived to have high scores on Baldwin's Afrocentric personality scale. The theory of an optimal conceptual system developed by Linda Myers was used to ascertain if the worldview of the organization is Afrocentric. Myers previously mentioned a list of assumptions that are evident in the optimal conceptual system which was incorporated in the study of the Shrine. Also, The Afrocentric organizational model presented by Schiele is relevant to the study because the Shrine of the Black Madonna

views the individual as an element of the collective.

The Shrine of the Black Madonna is a Black Nationalist religious organization.

Its belief systems are reflected in the personality of its members. The members of this

organization have a collective identity within the organization which is reflected and

reinforced by the African saying, "I am because we are, because we are, therefore I am."

The survival thrust of the Shrine of the Black Madonna appears Afrocentric because the

organization practices communal economics, African religion, and culture.

Methodology

This study focuses on religious, economic, and cultural dynamics of the Shrine of

the Black Madonna. Two qualitative approaches were used to understand the

mechanisms used by this group. The researcher used interpretive research methods as

well as a critical research method. The results of the study can be used to recommend

strategies to attack economic, political, and cultural problems that prevent Africans in

America from fully developing their communities. The researcher will share this

knowledge with religious groups within the African community. Secondly, this study

investigates whether an organization, such as the Shrine of the Black Madonna,

influences and even creates Afrocentric personalities. The Shrine also teaches people of

African descent to know themselves through the study of their history. Thirdly, the

indoctrination rituals are the focus of this study on of the Shrine of the Black Madonna.

These rituals help teach new members how to become responsible to the African people

that are a part of their nation. Thus, one of the outcomes of this study should result in demonstrating nationalism as a liberation strategy for organizations in their efforts to bring about the total independence for Africans in the Diaspora.

The methods used by the Shrine of the Black Madonna to convert individuals from simple Negroes to blacks or Africans were examined. The conversion experience measured the members' level of Afrocentricity. The researcher, through the use of surveys and interviews, examined the theories of Afrocentricity as the members of this group practice it. The use of a questionnaire was constructed from previous measurement constructs by African psychologists. The concept of self-knowledge is a variable that can be measured by studying how this organization creates Afrocentric personalities.

The concept of Afrocentricity was measured to understand what role the organization played in the development of personalities that act as agents of the Black Liberation Movement within the black community. This was done through interactions with members utilizing the research strategy of participant observation and by presenting the ideas of the leaders and founders. The interviews of leaders focused on their ideas as a possible reflection a theory of Afrocentricity.

The primary role of this study is to investigate a specific Afrocentric organization and the means utilized to engage theory as practice. There is a mass of available literature on the Afrocentric personalities of the black communities; but studies of such an organization are limited. The reason for studying this organization is to ascertain the ways that black people can use the knowledge internalized pertaining to an Afrocentric survival thrust to liberate themselves.

The method used in this dissertation is the mixed method approach. The mixed method approach is one in which the researcher tends to base knowledge claims on programmatic grounds, or problem centered. It employs strategies of inquiry that involve collecting data either simultaneous or sequentially to best understand research problems. The data collection also involves gathering both numeric information (e.g. on instruments) as well as text information (e.g. on interviews) so that the final database represents both quantitative and qualitative information. A mixed method design was used because it captures the best of both quantitative and qualitative approaches.[30]

Mixed Methods

The mixed method approach was used in this study. The data collection was sequential. There were multiple forms of data employing all possibilities, using statistical and text analyses. The data collection and analysis were integrated at the data analysis stage.

The qualitative data were the major emphasis. The interviews and observations were used with the surveys to assess the effect of policy and program on members and whether or not the members are Afrocentric in their personalities.

Sequential Exploratory Strategy

The sequential exploratory strategy was conducted in two phases with the priority given to the qualitative data. The qualitative data consisted of interviews and participant observation. The analysis was of data collected from both methods. The integration occurs in the interpretation of data in the discussion section of this dissertation.[31] Figure

---

[30] John W. Creswell, *Qualitative Inquiry and Research Design: Choosing among Five Approaches*, 3rd ed. (Los Angeles: Sage Publication 2003), 156.

[31] Ibid., 21.

1 presents the sequential exploratory design of this study. This approach was chosen because it allowed the researcher an opportunity to explore the phenomenon of how members of the Shrine assumed an African-based thrust for living in America.

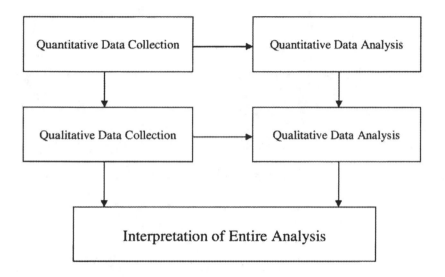

Figure 1. Sequential Exploratory Design

The researcher also used the technique of non-random sampling by getting involved with known members and did not interview people who have left the organization. New members were interviewed to determine what facet of the organization interested them initially. The methods used to attract new members were also researched. Non-traditional methods have been shown to attract specific types of individuals within the black community. In his book, *The Autobiography of Malcolm X*,

Malcolm X described a recruitment process of the Nation of Islam known as "fishing

for converts."[32]

Surveys, interviews, and questionnaires were the instruments utilized for this

study. The researcher also recorded his observations as data to place into his analysis of

data obtained. The researcher interviewed members of the Shrine of the Black Madonna

in Atlanta, Georgia. The survey and questionnaire targeted the same members as

respondents. The interviews were performed with the researcher asking specific

questions of the leaders of the group. The researcher used prior methodologies referred

to by Baldwin and Schiele. The investigator also focused on the contributions of the

founders of this organization. The researcher obtained permission from leaders to

interview them as well as their members. The participating leaders in the study and the

other participants were given prior knowledge of the purpose of the study and the usage

of the obtained results. The researcher participated in the rituals as he observed the

practices of the organizations activities.

Observation/Participant Methodology

The methodology for the observation/participant part of the study consisted of

field notes and on-site observations. The on-site observation of the Shrine's cultural

center and Holocaust museum was completed with the cooperation of the center's

manager as the guide.

---

[32] Alex Haley, *The Autobiography of Malcolm X*, (New York: Ballantine Books, 1964), 224.

The field notes were taken during the researcher's visit to the Beulah Land Farm. The field notes from the observation of the worship service were used to study the members in their church activities. The researcher participated in the history class and used the class experience as the basis for his observation.

Quantitative Methods

The population for this study was members of the Shrine of the Black Madonna. There are 500 members of the Shrine which is situated in the West End community of Atlanta. The Chief Executive of the Shrine consented to have members take the survey at the church or shrine. The sampling design is a single stage design. The people were sampled directly.

The individuals interviewed volunteered to do so after service at the Shrine where they were assembled. Each individual, up to 50, was selected and was chosen based on his or her availability at the Shrine. The site for the questionnaires is the sanctuary of the Shrine of the Black Madonna in Atlanta. The survey instrument is Kobi Kambon's African Self- Consciousness Scale. The ASC Scale is a 42-item personality questionnaire conceptually organized around four competency dimensions of African Self-Consciousness and six manifest dimensions based on some major categories of African social experiences. The four competencies are:

1. Awareness, recognition of one's collective African identity and heritage.

2. General ideology and activity placed on African survival, liberation and proactive affirmative development.

3. Specific activity priorities placed on African self-knowledge, African-centered values, ritual customs and institutions.

4. A posture of resistance toward anti-African forces and threats to African survival in general.[33]

The six manifest dimensions cover the area of education, family, religion, cultural activities, interpersonal relationships and political orientation. The internal validity of the ASC Scale has been established through several methods. The first use of Kambon's and Bell's scale was with students at an HBCU who were tested on 10. ASC characteristics which yielded a coefficient of Rho = 48 (p<-.001). The second use indicated a correlation between the ASC Scale and Robert Williams Black personality questionnaire[34] which yielded a coefficient of R=70.

Finally, factor analysis of the ASC Scale has yielded three rather than the four characteristics measured by the researcher. The underlying factors revealed: (1) a sense of collective African identity, (2) value for Afrocentric institutions, and (3) value for African survival and defense against anti-African threats. These three factors encompass the four augment theories: Test, retest, reliability, coefficient covering interviews from six weeks up to nine months occurred well within the high 1980s to low 1990s range. Research conducted with the ASC Scale has both its internal and external validity with most of the data falling within the former rather than the latter category.[35]

A sample item from the ASC Scale is as follows: (1) Blacks who trust Whites are very intelligent beings. The scales are 1 = very strongly disagree, 2 = strongly

---

[33] *Ibid.*, 162.

[34] K.K. Kambon, *The African Personalities in America*, 160.

[35] Ibid., 160.

disagree, 3 = moderate disagree, 4 = slightly disagree, 5 = slightly agree, 6 = moderately agree, 7 = strongly agree, 8 = very strongly agree. There are no right or wrong answers.

The independent variable in this study is African-centered consciousness. The four dependent variables would be the four competencies identified by Kobi K. Kambon:

1. Collective African Identity and Self Fortification

2. Resistance toward anti-African forces

3. Priority of African centered institutions and cultural expression

4. African cultural preferences.

Qualitative Methods

The qualitative section of the study used open-ended questions to elicit the policy implementations of the program of the Shrine of the Black Madonna. Ten participants were interviewed at the Shrine. The people interviewed were selected from the top leaders to the primary group leaders. A list of ten questions is included in the findings. The open-ended observations were completed at the Shrine and at the Beulah Land Farm. The observation was of the service at the Shrine, the history class, and the projects and land at the farm. The researcher used the photographs taken while observing these sites. The researcher has been attending the Shrine for several years and is familiar with the site and the leadership personnel.

The Shrine has been in Atlanta since the late 1970s and the researcher first attended the Shrine in 1978. The Shrine has brought Afrocentric techniques to the black church community in Atlanta. It has been involved in community projects to improve the life and quality of cultural activities in the community. The advent of African liberation day is the celebration of Malcolm X's and Marcus Garvey's birthdays. The Shrine has also participated and organized these cultural holy days.

The Shrine was convenient for the researcher and the participants as a site for the interviews. The shrine administrators were informed of the intention of the researcher and were very cooperative. The researcher participated in the observation at the Shrine. The interviews were face-to-face and were recorded on audio tape. The researcher used the ethnographic approach in which the Shrine was studied in its natural setting over a period of time.

Significance of the Study

This study is based on the premise that Afrocentric organizations will produce Afrocentric personalities that are able to eradicate most of the problems that people in the African community confront on a daily basis. In addition, psychologists and social scientists have studied the Afrocentric personalities, but there are few studies on organizations to determine if they are Afrocentric or not. The main outcome should be that organizations, which possess an Afrocentric worldview, should be composed of members that have Afrocentric personalities. The study also shows how this organization tries to remake the world in African images.

The methods used by this researcher were a combination of the qualitative and quantitative approaches in an effort to collect data. The study incorporates the use of surveys, interviews, questionnaires, and the observations of the researcher. The interpretive perspective was used with a critical social perspective. The researcher visited the organization in Atlanta, Georgia. The scope of the organization's programs was recorded in reports. Members of this organization were offered the opportunity to give a personal view of the philosophies and programs of their organization.

Religion in the African community is an important aspect of daily life. In America, blacks are apt to join any social organization, but they must acknowledge God in their activities. When black people formally meet, it is common to often begin or end the meeting with a prayer. Black churches are places that instill a sense of the importance of God in many black people's lives. The researcher participated in the ceremonies and activities of the organization to determine the effects of the organization's use of symbols. The fact that the Shrine of the Black Madonna uses African languages in its practices, it gives a different perspective from most Christian church practices and rituals as well. The groups' activities were used to determine if these organizations have Afrocentric objectives during the socialization of their members. The researcher used quota sampling to determine the range of generation participation. New organizations tend to attract younger people because they are generally more open to new ideas.

The Shrine of the Black Madonna used a system of open socialization in the 1970s and 1980s. Now, however, they are seldom seen in the street. At some point, a change of tactics occurred. The researcher attempted to investigate the new strategies.

The patriarchs who founded the organization are now dead. This paper attempts to measure how the organization continues to keep the members that were inspired after the death of the spiritual founder. The context from which these organizations developed was also investigated. The researcher has a conceptual thesis of what the cause of the context was.

The Shrine of the Black Madonna arose out of a historical development in the African-American Community. The conditions of slavery created dysfunctional and alien models that left Africans with a Eurocentric psychological framework. A Eurocentric consciousness was instilled in Africans to perpetuate the oppressive slave condition. Both the Shrine and the Nation of Islam have techniques to help deconstruct the alien concepts and instill in each individual African consciousness.

This study focuses on the process of constructing African personalities out of the imbedded alien consciousness. The religious organizations that preceded them failed to perform this task properly. The African model that the Shrine of the Black Madonna group uses was developed and based upon an African cosmology or worldview. The researcher looked to confirm this assumption through the use of behavior tests and questionnaires to measure Afrocentric personalities. The Afrocentric model that this organization is constructed was observed in action.

Summary

The Shrine of the Black Madonna arose out of historical development in the African-American community. The Shrine was a response to the conditions of a besieged community and the breakdown of African institutions that had created a functioning cosmology to maintain and sustain the African people. The condition of slavery created dysfunctional and alien models that left Africans with a suboptimal psychological framework. The optimal or African worldview promulgated the maintenance and sustenance of the African people at its center. Afrocentrism is an alternative perspective to the conditioning that supports the service of European-American interests. The

European suboptimal or Eurocentric consciousness was instilled into Africans to perpetuate the oppressive slave condition.

This alien psychological perspective caused the breakdown of the Afrocentric personality as well as its supporting institutions and traditions. The memory of African language, traditions and values were destroyed; thus, Africans lost possession of their historical continuity. They were taught to believe that they were Negroes and that they did not have a history. The European created the personality that was alienated from its African cosmology by destroying the African model that blacks developed in their native civilizations. The African-American experienced a holocaust, which took them from their belief in themselves to violence against self, brainwashing, and conditioning. The African came to accept the Eurocentric view of themselves.

The conversion experience of African-Americans in organizations that restore the self-knowledge, dignity, and African-centered view of the self is reflected in the ideology, philosophy, and practice of the Shrine of the Black Madonna. Black organizations that use an African cosmology model and true African history produce Afrocentric personalities. The Shrine of the Black Madonna operates based on African principles which presuppose that the person is not just an individual, but also a member of a collective group. The communal values of the black people which were destroyed by the European during the Diaspora are restored in these organizations through group identification. The European worldview is illuminated by the poem by the Native American Sitting Bull, written in 1877, at the Powder Run Council.

> Yet hear me my people. We now have to deal with another race. Small and feeble when our fathers first met them, but now they are great and overbearing. Strangely enough, they have a mind to till the soil. And the love of possession is

a disease with them. These people have many laws that the rich may break but the poor may not. They claim this mother of ours, the Earth, as their own, and fence their neighbors away. They deface her with their buildings and their refuse. That nation is like a spring freshet that overruns its bank and destroys all who are in its path.[36]

Franz Fanon states "I feel within myself a soul as immense as the world, a master being forced to adopt the humility of a slave."[37]

Organization of the Dissertation

This dissertation is divided into five chapters. Chapter I is the introduction and it includes an overview of the dissertation. Chapter II presents a detailed review of the literature related to the study. Chapter III offers an historical review of the Shrine of the Black Madonna. The findings and discussion of the findings are presented in Chapter IV. Chapter V presents the conclusion and recommendations for future research.

Definition of Terms

African-Centered: At the center of African History with African people as the subject of history and no longer objects of European history, and they are agents of their own history.

Afrocentric/Africentric: The African-American worldview that uses Africa as its subject and center of reference.

Afrocentric Model: The model that conceives individual identity as part of a collective. That is, the person is the total of his ancestors before him, his personality, and those that are yet unborn.

Afrocentric Organizational Model: The organizational model that places the organization and group survival above material productivity.

---

[36] Linda J. Myers, *Understanding an Afrocentric Worldview* (Dubuque, IA: Kendall/Hunt publication, 1998), 27.

[37] Frantz Fanon, *Black Skin, Black Mask* (New York: Grove Press, 1967), 40.

Afrocentric Paradigm: Predicated on traditional African philosophical assumptions that emphasize the interconnectedness and interdependence of natural phenomena. There is no demarcation between the spiritual and material, substance and form.

Afrocentric Personality: The African-American view of a holistic personality, which is the healthy person, grounded in the African idea of Sudicism.

Afrocentrism: The welfare of the group takes precedence over the welfare of the individual, the philosophy about which the subject of inquiry is African.

Black/African: A person of African descent.

Collective Identity: The individual considers himself not as a separate entity, but as a part of the whole community: "I am because we are, and because we are, therefore I am."

Optimal: The functioning behavior that maintains and affirms a consciousness framed by the following characteristics: holistic, non-materialistic, and communal orientation.

Sub-optimal – the worldview that individualism, competition and materialism provide criteria for self-definition. As a natural consequence of this finite and limited focus, one orients toward such disorder that one fights others to sustain an illusion.

Sudicism: The African idea of harmony in the universe; the spiritual commitment to an ideological view of harmony.

CHAPTER II

REVIEW OF THE LITERATURE

Historical Overview of the Research Literature

The concept of Afrocentricity developed by Molefi Kete Asante began a

revolution of the study of the African personality. Asante was not the first person of

African descent to study African people from an African perspective. However, he did

consolidate Afrocentric ideas. He began with *David Walker's Appeal* and Delaney's *The*

Condition, Elevation, Emigration, and Destiny of the Colored People of the United

States. This literature was republished in 1993 and they each synthesized the

nationalistic view of these revolutionaries. Walker and Delaney presented the idea that

Africans in the U.S. were from the African continent, therefore they possessed an African

personality.[1]

Marcus Garvey's ideas from the early twentieth century were also a foundation

that formed a partial basis for Asante's concept of Afrocentricity. Garvey's contribution

was his coordination of blacks into forming cooperative businesses that aimed to create

an economic base for the liberation of blacks in the U.S. and Africa.

Asante also incorporated many of the contributions of Elijah Muhammad and

Malcolm X; they were key leaders of the Black Muslim movement of the 1960s. It was

during the 1960s when Malcolm X developed the idea of black consciousness. After that

time, the Afrocentric personality was given form and substance. Malcolm X, in his

---

[1] Asante, *Afrocentricity*, 22.

speeches, propagated an African worldview that reflected the centrality of Africa. In the

book, *Autobiography of Malcolm X*, Malcolm explains how an Afrocentric personality is

given birth.[2]

Albert Cleage, Jr., the founder of the Shrine of the Black Madonna, was a

contemporary of Malcolm X. Rev. Cleage's ideas of Black Christian Nationalism were

based on two specific concepts that remain central to the concepts of the Madonna

organization. These two concepts were communal economics (Ujamaa) and collective

unity (Ujima). Asante describes the basis of Afrocentricity in his 1980 book,

Afrocentricity. He states:

> The Ancient African civilization did not separate religion and philosophy.
> Indeed, the contributions to Art, Literature and the Sciences are directly
> traceable to the Nile Valley civilizations. Expressions of this unity of religion
> and philosophy appeared in the construction of Temples, Memorials, Obelisks,
> Causeways, and Pyramids of the Classical Period.[3]

Asante describes the contributions of Elijah Muhammad as objectivism.

> Like Marcus Garvey, Elijah Muhammad was an effective organizer who readily
> grasped our economic realities. He knew that consumerism could not provide
> economic autonomy, and so he also aimed to control production. H is for 'Help
> Yourself,' a program that provided a corrective measure for the liberation of
> African Americans from the years of sleep in the Land of Plenty.[4]

However, Elijah Muhammad also taught that the black man must know himself. He put

forth the idea of the black man as the first man. These two concepts shocked blacks into

a realization of their Africanness and the beauty of blackness.

---

[2] Haley, *The Autobiography of Malcolm X*, 20.

[3] Molefi Kete Asante, *Kemet, Afrocentricity and Knowledge* (Trenton, NJ: Africa World Press Inc., 1990), 190.

[4] Ibid., 22.

The concept of Afrocentricity is clearly stated in Asante's passage:

"Afrocentricity is a mode of thought and action in which the centrality of African interests, values and perspectives predominates. In regards to theory, it is the placing of an African people in the center of any analysis of African phenomena."[5] There have been many other theories focusing on the Afrocentric personality since Asante first introduced his concept. There is J.A. Baldwin's theory of the Afrocentric personality. This theory is relevant to this present study because its final conclusion shows that the Afrocentric personality has a survival thrust and propagates nation building maintenance.

Linda Myers' theory of the optimal worldview in her book, *Understanding an Afrocentric Worldview*, is also part of the expansion of the Afrocentric concept. Myers defines her view as a womanist perspective, or from the perspective of African womanism. She further states, "A conceptual system is the structure of philosophical assumptions and principles on which a way of viewing the world is based; of the conceptual systems we shall examine, one is fragmented and assumes that the transphysical and physical (spirit and matter) are separate."[6] Her other view is holistic—assuring the unity of the spirit and matter—has then oneness; the latter is an Afrocentric worldview. This is the researcher's historical sketch of the development of the Afrocentric worldview.

---

[5] Ibid., 2.

[6] Linda J. Myers, *Understanding An Afrocentric Worldview* (Dubuque, IA: Kendall/Hunt Publishing Co., 1988), 16.

Discussion of Literature Specific to the Dissertation Topic

The Afrocentric personality is internalized in the Nation of Islam and the Shrine of the Black Madonna. The conversion experience of these nationalist organizations is rooted in their Afrocentric worldviews. The applicable Afrocentric organizational theory is offered by Janice D. Hamlet who published an article in the book *Afrocentric Visions*. It is entitled "Rethinking Organizations from an Afrocentric Viewpoint." Hamlet discusses the two organizational theories as follows: the limited conception of human identity found in the Eurocentric model is reflected in the way the client is conceived in human service organizational theory evidenced throughout the human service organization literature. The client is usually conceived as one individual, as if she or he lives in a vacuum and is not part of a social group.[7] Hamlet, T. Cook, and R. Koni stated that in black or African psychology, individuality in the sense of self in opposition to the group disappears and is replaced by a common goal.[8] Moreover, Asante's concept of experiential commonality or the sharing of a particular experience by a particular group of people and Baldwin's 1981 concept of African self-consciousness are important in understanding a fundamental characteristic of Afrocentrism, which places emphasis on discerning and de-emphasizing individual differences.[9] Afrocentrism gives preeminence to the group as opposed to the individual. The welfare of the group takes precedence over the welfare of the individual.

---

[7] Janice D. Hamlet, *Rethinking Organizations from an Afro centric Viewpoint, Afrocentric Visions*, Ed. Janice D. Hamlet (London: Sage Publications, 1998), 76.

[8] Ibid., 73.

[9] Ibid., 12.

There is very little literature that applies the Afrocentric model to an organization but there is considerable literature regarding the individual and the group. Hamlet has applied this theory to the organizational model by employing the Afrocentric paradigm.[10] Linda J. Myers' optimal worldview theory is important to understanding how Afrocentric conceptual theory affects the personalities of persons belonging to Afrocentric organizations and those who do not. Myers asserts:

> Individualism, competition, and materialism provided criteria for self definition as a natural consequence of a worldview in which a finite and limited focus orients us toward such disorder that we fight one another to sustain an illusion. This is the result of the suboptimal worldview. The pain, insecurity, guilt, fear, anxiety, and destruction of the suboptimal worldview usually creates an alternative (optimal) worldview in order to return to peace, harmony, collaboration and the good of all.[11]

The alternative is the Afrocentric or optimal worldview. Myers goes on further to summarize this as:

> Consciousness that permeating essence, or pervasive energy, or spirit, plays a primary role. In African thought the role and importance of consciousness is evidenced in concepts such as Mdw Ntr (Divine Speech) and Nommo (power of the word). The conceptual system is described as optimal because it is structured toward the achievement of everlasting peace and happiness.[12]

The Nation of Islam's ideology of separation of the races has tenets that are similar to the ideas of the Shrine of the Black Madonna; whereas, in the NOI, the Black Muslims demand absolute separation of the black and white races. The Shrine is willing to approach this goal by stages. The economic and political links, for example, need not be

---

[10] Ibid., 13.

[11] Linda J. Myers, *Understanding the Afro centric Worldview* (Dubuque: Kendall/Hunt Publishing Co., 1988), 11.

[12] Ibid., 13.

severed immediately, but all personal relationships between the races must be broken now. However, only with complete racial separation will the perfect harmony of the universe be restored.[13] This facet of the Shrine's belief-system establishes a situation within the groups (blacks) where a person is immersed in black culture. The present crisis, involving the black man's struggle for survival in America, demands the resurrection of a black church with its own black messiah. Only this kind of a Black Christian Church can serve as the unifying center for the totality of the black man's life and struggle. Only this kind of a Black Christian Church can reinforce each individual black man's choice of where he will stand: united with his own people and laboring and sacrificing in the spirit of the Black Messiah or individually seeking his own advancement and maintaining his slave identification with the white oppressor.[14] These two tenets set the stage from which these organizations convert their members into a black culture committed to an African worldview.

Research in Cognate Areas Relevant to the Topic Under Investigation

Nga Oyo A. Kwate's research is relevant to the cognate area. He integrates the works of all the current Afrocentric theories in his article, "Cross Validation of Afrocentrism Scale," published in the *Journal of Black Psychology*. He maintains, "Thus for individuals of African descent, optimal functioning has been described as behavior

---

[13] C. Eric Lincoln, *The Black Muslims in America* (New York: Koyode Publications LTD, 1961), 91.

[14] Albert Cleage Jr., *The Black Messiah* (Trenton, NJ: Africa World Press, 1989), 9.

that maintains and affirms a consciousness framed by these characteristics."[15] For

example, Myers defined an optimal Afrocentric belief system, as one characterized by a

holistic, non materialistic, and communal orientation. Others contend that normal

functioning in Africans is expressed as oneness and harmony with nature, communal

phenomenology, spiritualistic transcendency, and collective survival thrust.[16]

However, taken together, the Afrocentric or Africentric worldview affirms and

promotes the sustenance, growth, and liberation of people of African descent. This

means that on the cognitive plane, Afrocentricity requires a black mindset. William

Cross, Jr. summarized a paper entitled, "The Thomas and Cross Models of Psychological

Nigrescence."[17] This paper cites the Thomas and Cross models on psychological

Nigrescence, and reviews the empirical studies that have been conducted to validate the

models. Nigrescence means the process of becoming black, and as black Americans have

traversed in seeking a more authentic identity during the late 1960s and early 1970s; this

model in effect speaks to the psychology of becoming black. In the broader sense, these

formulations focus on the human drama of adult identity transformation within the

context of a social movement or revitalization movement. The Black Power Movement

of the 1960s and 1970s refocused the black psyche to emphasize and extol its blackness.

Naim Akbar, in his book, *Know Thy Self*, describes an African concept of

personality. Akbar further indicates there is a "definition" of self:

---

[15] Nga Oyo A. Kwate, "Cross-Validation of the Afrocentrism Scale," *Journal of Black Psychology* 29 (August 2003): 301-324.

[16] Ibid, 308-324.

[17] Kambon, K.K., *African Black Psychology*, 289.

> The African Self is a multidimensional occurrence that is represented within the individual person, but also transcends the individual; it is in the present but also transcends time . . . In order for us to obtain knowledge of self, one does not simply gain insight into ones individual ego and its experience but instead, the self is considered in this holistic way that ultimately encompasses the entire cosmos.[18]

The African concept of self is comprised of the soul, breath of life, the body, the physical self, the mind, the personal self, the social, relational, and the tribal and ancestral self. The one view of the self is the soul in the African traditional concept of self. It is the spiritual that one is endowed with from the Creator or God. This is the Ba—or Breath of life which runs through all humans and it is universal. Its origin is from the Creator of the universe. In the African cosmos, the idea of Creator is essential in the African idea of self. However, this is not the case with Western psychology in its concept of the personality. The Eurocentric view of the personal self is the major idea in Western psychology. Sigmund Freud's view of the self includes three elements, the id, ego, and super ego. Akbar uses this framework while describing the African personal self.

The gender of the African concept of personality is seen as complementary and that there are many ways to express ones gender. All men and all women are not alike. Education about gender is the result of formal learning experiences and social interaction. Gender should not be borrowed from a foreign concept of gender; therefore, the African concept of gender is not left to chance. The African concept of gender has been explained through African Rites of Passage for boys and girls. The Egyptians' idea of gender is considered to be one of the seven souls of humans. People are born into gender, and it is considered to be driven and determined upon conception. Akbar states

---

[18] Naim Akbar, *Know Thy Self* (Tallahassee, FL: Mind Productions and Associates 1998), 18.

that western concepts of gender are not correct for Africans. He maintains that "It is significant that most African cultures have instruction that is specialized for young men and women to explore and discover their way to express their masculinity or femininity."[19] The mis-education in the Eurocentric educational system presumes superiority of one gender over the other. This is not the African way.

Critical Analysis of Appropriate Research Literature

The critical analysis begins with Asante's concepts painful demise of Eurocentrism. Asante posits that:

> Now the demise of Eurocentrism is necessary because it structures a set of values and insists on a framework that views Africa and Africans in a junior light. This is a formula for constant intellectual revolt and physical violence; one must choose either to engage in a legitimate quest for mutuality or an inevitable struggle for dominance.[20]

The main point of this research is to affirm that Afrocentric idea and concepts as defined by Asante, Myers, Baldwin, Hamlet, and other scholars in reevaluating the contribution of the Nation of Islam and the Shrine of the Black Madonna in undoing the destruction of the African mind by Eurocentrism in America.

Asante credits Cheikh Anta Diop as a primary figurehead in reversing Eurocentrism on the African continent. Asante has done the same in the United States. Diop, the late Senegalese scholar, was the dominant Afrocentric thinker of the twentieth century. Although his works readily gained acceptance in the United States after he was introduced to the scholarly community by the lectures and papers of John Henrik Clark, it

---

[19] Ibid., 28.

[20] Molefi Kete Asante, *The Painful Demise of the Euro centrism* (Trenton, NJ: African World Press, 1999), X.

has taken much longer for Diop to make the same impact on the African continent. Struggling against the entrenched orthodoxy of the Eurocentric analysis of Africa, Diop almost single handedly turned the intellectual tables on a tradition that, for the most part, had seen Africa as a object of the European experience.[21] Asante illustrates the contribution of Diop to the endeavor of black womanism.

> Cheikh Anta Diop's attempt to solve another part of the puzzle of African historiography, that is, the origin and nature of African unity, led to the original publication of the Cultural Unity of Black Africa. Thus, as he had done originally in earlier works, Diop takes on leading European thinkers in an attempt to show the inadequacy of their arguments in relationship to the idea of matriarchy. He makes a straightforward case against the writings of J.J. Bachefen, LM. Morgan, and F. Engels. This is the first time that he confronts the patriarchy designed by Europeans to support male dominance.[22]

Thus, Diop's advances play a role in Asante's basis for his Afrocentric theories. Asante gives Diop credit in his book, *The Painful Demise of Eurocentrism.*[23]

This research topic is an attempt to apply an Afrocentric theory to deal with a black organization. Black institutions that operate from the sub-optimal worldview of Euro- centrism must be replaced with the ideas of the optimal worldview of Afrocentrism. Linda Myers view of optimal theory is the feminist side or affective sense where the Afrocentrism of the subject has a spiritual view of the world. The Afrocentric personality construct by J. A. Baldwin can be extended to include the concept of Maat, or justice, balance, as personified by the goddess Maat.

---

[21] Ibid.

[22] Ibid., XI.

[23] Ibid., X.

The Afrocentric focus must create a just society ruled by the male or female principles in every area of society. J. A. Baldwin's concept of Eurocentrism is expressed in the following statement, "One could say a basic emphasis in the European structure is toward exclusiveness. The basic theme characterizing European cosmology is that of man versus nature; conflict and antagonism, with the emphasis being on man's mastery and control over nature through domination oppression, aggression and unnatural alteration."[24] Baldwin uses the Afrocentric theory to analyze the relationships of African-Americans male and females. Therefore, once people free themselves of this dominance of male over female, then the harmony of the male or female principle results in a more peaceful world.

Summary

The Afrocentric worldview of the Nation of Islam and the Shrine of the Black Madonna reflect what Asante observes as the centrality of Africa. Asante states that the Africans being seen as subjects instead of as objects in the concept of Afrocentrism is essential. These two organizations were reviewed to show how the collective unity, communal economics, and culture have created an optimal worldview that promotes Afrocentric personalities, centrally concerned with the liberation of black people. The demise of Eurocentrism will bring forth a new beginning in the history of Africans. This period has been referred to as the Beginning Again, or B.A. after 1625. The African

---

[24] J. A. Baldwin, *Afrocentric Cultural Consciousness and African American, Afrocentric Visions*, Ed. Janice D. Hamlet (London: Sage Publications, 1998), 73.

Renaissance that Cheikh Anta Diop referred to in his book, *Toward the African Renaissance,* has come into existence in the concepts of Afrocentricity.[25] This provides an impetus to create the world in the image of Africans for Africans.

Contributions of this Study to the Literature

This study began the venture of research into the institutions created by Africans to remake the world in the images of Africans. It opens the area of research that has previously been limited to the Afrocentric personalities and Afrocentric groups to the area of Afrocentric organizational models that will develop counter institutions in the African community. African studies must look to serve the institutional needs of the communities in which they are found. The contributions of the Nation of Islam and the Shrine of the Black Madonna to the African community will be added to the literature of the Afrocentric enterprise. The ideology of Diop pertaining to African political ideology is a useful aspect for this purpose, because the research in this dissertation has political implications. The organizations that it will focus on have a political aim; the liberation of African peoples. Diop further states:

> In our struggle for national independence, a struggle that all oppressed people must wage to the last man, the primary objective is to create awareness among all Africans about Black Africa. By awareness, I mean a pioneering commitment which will bring every single African, from the Sahara to the Cape, from the city dweller (laborer, artisan, opinion leader; civil servant) to the country dweller; from the Muslim to the Christian and disciples of paleonegritic religions, to realize:
>
> 1. That they must fight for ideas and not for persons.
>
> 2. That the fate of a people is first and foremost in its own hands.

---

[25] Cheikh Anta Diop, *Toward the African Renaissance,* (London: Karnac House, 1996), 45.

3. That their fate does not depend essentially on the assertive eloquence of some deputy in some European House of Assembly.

4. That this fate can be improved here on Earth by natural means. Such means have proved successful for other peoples. Humanity can transform society and nature.

5. That in practice, these natural means are a collective struggle organized and adopted to life circumstances (strike by sellers of agricultural products; consumer's strikes sponsored by organized cooperatives, hunger strike, political strike, petitions, delegations, boycotts, arousing international opinion,: other mass movements like local demonstrations at continental level so as this is possible.[26]

Thus, Africa must unite Africans at home and abroad. The call for the liberation of African people is the survival thrust of the Nation of Islam and the Shrine of the Black Madonna and is a main goal of this study.

The crucial difference between the theories of the first variety non-Afrocentric theories and those of the second Afrocentric theories is that the non-Afrocentric theories former tend to conceptualize the black personality as the essential net result of Western oppression (i.e. emphasis on the Western or European reality in the nature and operation of black personality). The black personality consists of a core system called the African Self-extension Orientation and African Self-consciousness with a number of basic traits emanating from the core. A black personality, modeled by Joseph Baldwin, points out two levels of the diagram that illustrate components of the black personality that he thinks differs from the European personality. In the Shrine of the Black Madonna, the black personality is formed on the self-consciousness level by the church giving an relevant African image that is worshiped as God or Orisha and the Netcher as being

---

[26] Ibid., 47.

represented as black models. Jesus is looked upon as a black revolutionary spirit that is reborn with each generation of the Black Nation.

The concept of Jesus being God's son and being white is considered White Nationalism. The Shrine practices knowledge of self, through teaching the true history of Jesus and African people in general. According to black nationalism, both God and Jesus are black. The black nation is viewed upon as God's chosen people because they choose to be his children. Black people in the Shrine are taught values that promote the black survival thrust articulated by Baldwin. The main objective of the Shrine is black liberation.[27]

In his article, "Organizational Theory from an Afrocentric Perspective," Jerome H. Schiele states his purpose:

> This article seeks to contribute to the study of Afrocentric concepts and issues (i.e. apology) and to highlight the world view of African people in the context of organizational theory. The Afrocentric paradigm predicated on traditional African philosophical assumptions that emphasize the interconnectedness and interdependence of natural phenomena.[28]

The tenets that reflect an African centered perspective of the human science model or conceptual paradigms are the following:

1. Human beings are conceived collectively.

2. Human beings are good.

3. Human beings are spiritual.

---

[27] Joseph A. Baldwin, African Self-Consciousness and the Mental Health of African-Americans, *Journal Black Studies* 15, no.2, (December 1984): 180.

[28] Jerome H. Schiele, Organizational Theory from Afrocentric Perspective, *Journal of Black Studies 21*, no. 2 (December 1990): 149.

4. The effective approach to knowledge is epistemologically valued.

5. Much of human behavior is irrational.

6. The axiology or highest values lie in interpersonal relations.[29]

Jerome Schiele identifies Afrocentric scholars such as Baldwin, Asante, and Nobles as individuals who differ about the Afrocentric model of an organization or group tenets which reflect the fact that the group's welfare takes precedence over the individual's welfare. At the Shrine of the Black Madonna, the individual is conceived of collectively. The saying in the Afrocentric community when it comes to organizations is that there is no room for individuals in organizations.[30]

Schiele also states that in addition to the Afrocentric model's concept of survival, the boundaries of the organization and extend into the community. This focus highlights organizational community relations more strongly than any existing human service organization theory. Just as it is unthinkable to understand the individual as separate from the others in the Afrocentric model, so it is unthinkable to understand the organization separate from the community which it serves.[31]

The black personality described by Clark, McGee, Nobles and Luther X in the article, "Voodoo or IQ: An Introduction of African Psychology," is one grounded in Euro-American reality. The African concept of man at its core (soul) or spiritual entity is propose for the African to have a religious perspective that causes him to survive slavery,

---

[29] Ibid., 147.

[30] Ibid., 149.

[31] Ibid., 150.

post-slavery, and the recent era of segregation. The black personality, which has

ostensibly adjusted to Western society, is characterized by what Euro-American

psychologists would call a schizoid adjustment. This means that he lives in two worlds

which diametrically differ on many key dimensions.[32] The black personality attempts to

foster an image that is accepted by Europeans and also tries to function as his black

oppositions demands it to function. According to Cedric X, "The growing failure of such

schizoid adjustment has seen an increase of suicide rates among middle-class blacks as

well as the growing incidences of depression and general mal-contentment."[33]

Furthermore, in his article regarding some alternative strategies in African

personality research, Azibo discusses the definition of the African personality. He states:

> The African personality is defined by (1) recognition of oneself as African,
> (2) a corresponding psychological and behavior disposition to sustain and
> develop the extended African self, and (3) a disposition to neutralize or
> otherwise render harmless all people and things that are anti-African or anti-
> black. In other words, the natural and ordered African personality state is to
> engage in the African survival thrust. The African survival thrust behavior
> manifested by the ordered African personality is based on the strength of
> psychological Africanity or African self-consciousness.[34]

Therefore, this study used the definition developed by Baldwin and other scholars

to develop the type of personality to be studied in the religious group the Shrine of Black

Madonna and in the personality of its founder Reverend Albert Cleage. James Joseph

Baldwin's African Self-Consciousness Scale test was the instrument utilized to study

---

[32] Cedric X (Clark) et al, "Voodoo or IQ: An Introduction to African Psychology," *Journal of Black Psychology* 1, no. 2 (December(1975): 9-29.

[33] Ibid., 27.

[34] Daudi Ajani Ya Azibo, "Pitfalls and some Ameliorative Strategy in African Personality," *Journal of Black Studies 19, no. 3* (March 1989): 316.

Africans who undergo a transformation from their self-concept of being only an individual to being a collective. This group process is what creates a new Afrocentric personality that is greater than just the individual personality around which Western civilization revolves. What is a Kua group and how does it function in the Shrine's theology? The seven steps in the Kua group concept or process include the following:

Step One—Invocation: We acknowledge the presence of God. This step makes the group of seekers aware of the presence of God within the sacred circle and the need for God's healing power.

- Awareness of the presence of God
- Ringing of the Sacred Bells
- Call and Response
- Kutafuta meditative response
- Need for the Healing Power of God
- Prayer of Invocation, which is designed to call on God

Step Two—Discourse on the Nature of God and what God expects us to do: Covenant Relationship. The second step continually makes the group aware of the nature of God, and it defines our faith.

Step Three—We have failed to satisfy our Covenant Relationship with God. We are sinners! This step emphasizes that we are sinners because we have failed to satisfy our Covenant Relationship with God.

Step Four—Confession and Penance: Jaramoi says, admit guilt, pain and suffering. Admit repression; you do not know the cause of your pain. Renounce the slave culture and niggerization which enslaves us and binds us in chains to our pain and frustration.

1. Prayer of courage
2. Confession Encounter
3. Purification

Step Five—Awareness: To sharpen our perception which sharpens our perception of our relationship with God and with each other.

Step Six—We stimulate within (God incarnate) through massage/movements and a sense of communalism.

Step Seven—We open ourselves to the experience of God, which is mediation.

1. Guided Breathing
2. Chanting
3. Guided Meditation

Definition of God: God is cosmic energy and creative intelligence, the unified energy field in which we live, move, and have our being. The nature of God is therefore unified, harmonious and powerful.

Definition of Mankind: Mankind is created out of the same substance as God; therefore, we are energy because we are compressed energy, the systems within us are the inner divinity (God incarnate).

Definition of the Covenant: The conditions for Black Christian Nationalism is to be a people. The term "people" denotes unity and connectedness. "In order to be a people, we must be communal."

The Kua group phenomenon as practiced by the Shrine of the Black Madonna is this study's intended focus. By studying the Kua groups, the study will focus on how it changes the life of the members of the Shrine of the Black Madonna. These concepts are from the Shrine unpublished Handbook.[35]

Yurugu, by Marimba Ani, is referred to by a number of scholars such as Karenga, Baldwin and Azibo. Ani's use of the terms Asili, Utamawazo, and Utamaroho are defined in the introduction of her book *Yurugu.* Ani states in her present study that she has introduced the concept of Asili. A Kiswahili word that is used in several related ways to mean beginning, origin, source, nature, essence, and fundamental principal. Ani indicates that the Asili means seed, origin, and germ, (i.e. the source or initiating principal of development).[36]

Ani uses the term Asili as a conceptual tool to explain the European culture. The logic of how the Europeans culture works as well as how it developed as a culture. Ani

---

[35] Tenth Anniversary, Shrine #10, *National Tribute to Jeramogi Abebe Agyeman,* June 1987.

[36] Marimba Ani, *Yurugu* (Washington, DC: Nkoninfo Publications, 1994), 11.

also states that the Asili will enable us to understand and explain the behavior, thought, and creations of a people in terms of its logic and origin its culture. The European culture is examined using the Asili analysis.

Ani states that Asili is the primary determinative factor of cultural development and an essential explanatory principle of cultural theory. She borrowed two Kiswahili terms to understand the ideas of European cultural analysis. The scholar explains that Utamaduni means civilization or culture, Wazo means thought; Roho is spirit/life. Ani created the term Utamawazo to convey the idea of thought as determined by culture. She also introduced the term Utamaroho as the spirit life of a culture; and the collective personality of its members are the meanings she gives the term.

Ani identifies the central claim of European culture as universal, which is taken from a statement from Max Weber, "as we like to think." The key to the African centered answer lies in this statement, "as we like to think" which Ani said is the only element that is universal about western civilization.[37] Ani explains that its Utamaroho (we like) and its Utamawazo (to think) combined in a manner dictated by an Asili that causes the culture to consistently project itself in universalistic terms.

Thus, the problem is created in the relationship of European culture to other cultures in which the culture of the other (non white) is projected as primitive and inferior to the culture of the European. Europeans try to justify their imperialism on the premise that it is superior and that its own culture represents civilization. Therefore, its destruction of far more inferior cultures and peoples is justified based on the fact of the

---

[37] Ibid., 21.

idea of progress. Europeans do this through their presentation of a rationalistic religion they called Christianity, whereby the religion of the non-white peoples are said to be polytheistic and pagan, and thus must be conquered because Christianity is universal and superior. Ani explains that universalism in European thought is the translation of the omnipotent idea into a mental category, and ideological, and ethical mandates. All modes of the Utamawazo and ideology state the normality and imperative of universal form which creates the allusion of total control.[38]

Scientism is used for the European's desire for power. European Asili also strive for an ever expanding control. This is the basis of European culture. Its values must necessarily be presented as a system of universal values. Ani states, "As a single phenomenon, European cultural imperialism is the attempt to proselytize, encourage, and project European ideology. The Asili is imperialistic by definition. The cultural self is spread in order to control others, and by controlling other the culture spreads itself."[39]

Ani contends that the idea of recovery for non-European people of their culture is based on spiritualism as a vision of the human spirit. Then she states, "now that we have broken the power of their ideology, we must leave them and direct our energy toward the recreation of cultural alternatives informed by ancestral visions of a future that celebrates our Africaness and encourages the best of the human spirit."[40]

---

[38] Ibid., 566.

[39] Ibid., 567.

[40] Ibid., 570.

Steve Biko's ideas are relative to Marimba Ani's *Yurugu*, when he maintains that "The strongest weapon in the hands of the oppressor is the mind of the oppressed."[41] In addition, Kambon uses a cultural paradigm analysis that every person operates according to some group conception of reality and it is a conception which they have with other members of their reference group, the group with which they are identified (in terms of values, beliefs, custom, etc.). The group people identify with is usually their own indigenous cultural group under normal-natural circumstances. In the abnormal–unnatural circumstance, when people identify with an alien group conception of reality, they operate based on unnatural circumstances or their conception of reality is from an alien perspective. Kambon states that this analysis, therefore, argues that every person operates according to one cultural reality or another, depending on the culture with which they identify. Africans or other non-Europeans are those who live under the domination of foreign/European Eurasian cultures are usually the group of people who are offered this unnatural and abnormal condition of cultural misidentification.[42]

Many African Moslems have argued for quite some time that the distinct cultural and socio-environmental conditions of African and European people reflect a distinct racial cultural histories and fundamental difference in their natural make-up. The concept of cultural "Survival Thrust" is the one that Kambon employs to convey the meaning and role of human collective adaptation to their environment, and how that ongoing cumulative process actually defines their distinct collective histories and cultural

---

[41] Steve Biko, *I Write What I Like*, (London: Bowerdean Press, 1978), 68.

[42] Kambon, Kobi, K.K. African/Black Psychology in the American Context (Tallahassee, FL: Nubia Nation Publication 1998). 119.

philosophy of life. It represents adaptations which have advanced the survival for that particular group in its initial isolated biogenetic and environmental (geo-historical) conditions.[43]

Worldview is identified as the distinct unifying cosmological, ontological epistemological, and axiological concepts. These principles represent a racial cultural group natural cultural conceptual orientation and construction of reality. The four components of the worldview concept as presented by Kambon are as follows:

1. **Cosmology**: The cosmological component of worldview refers to the structure of reality from a particular racial cultural perspective, experience. African interdependence, culturalism, human-natural oneness, unity. European - separate/alienation, independence, human-nature conflict, control over nature.

2. **Ontology**: The ontological concept of worldview refers to the essence or essential nature of reality from a particular racial-cultural perspective/experience. African—a spiritual basis of nature/existence/the universe. European—a material basis of nature/experience/the universe.

3. **Axiology**: The axiological component of worldview refer to the basis nature system, defining relations between human and nature from a particular racial-cultural perspective/experience. African—emphasis on person to person, human to human relations. European—emphasis on person to person to object /human to object relations.

4. **Epistemology**: The epistemological component of worldview refers to the way or method of knowing or coming into an understanding of reality of what is real, from a particular racial-cultural perspective/experience. African—emphasis on affective cognitive, synthesis as the way of knowing reality. European—emphasis on cognitive over affective process as the way of knowing reality.[44]

---

[43] Ibid., 120.

[44] Ibid., 122.

Ama Mazama, author of *The Afrocentric Paradigm*, Africans do not exist on their own terms, but on those of Europeans. According to Mazama, people of African descent are dislocated, and having lost sight of themselves in the mist of Europeans decadence and madness, it becomes increasingly difficult for blacks to orient themselves in a positive and constructive manner, hence the plight of our people today.[45] Mazama contends that blacks' liberation rests on their ability to systematically displace European ways of thinking, being, feeling, so on and so forth…and consciously replace them with ways that are germane to their own African cultural experience. Furthermore, Mazama maintains that the Afrocentric idea rests upon the assertion of the primacy of the African experience for African people. Mazama identifies three aspects of the Afrocentric paradigm as the affective, cognitive, and conative. Mazama cites Karenga's idea of shared orientations of characteristics that pervade the Afrocentric paradigm. They are the following characteristics:[46]

1. The centrality of the community

2. Respect for tradition

3. A high level spirituality and ethical concern

4. Harmony with nature

5. The sociality of selfhood

6. Veneration of ancestors

7. Unity of being.

---

[45] Mazama, Ama, *The Afrocentric Paradigm* (Trenton, NJ: African World Press, 2003), 5.

[46] Ibid., 9.

Mazama examines the black nationalism of Marcus Garvey with the statement, "indomitable consciousness of victory that informs all of Garvey's philosophy makes it a truly powerful drives towards self determination, one that has moved millions of black people all over the world."[47]

The premises of Afrocentricity as Mazama defines them are the Marcus Garvey philosophy, the Negritude movement, and Karenga C. Diop's historiography and Fanonism. Frantz Fanon's ideas toward decolonization are that the colonized must use violence against the colonizer because the colonizer used violence against the colonized indigenous people of Africa. Fanon states that when colonized people kill their oppressors, they destroy the slaves and the masters at the same time. Mazama examines Fanonism in its most profound aspect, the liberation of Africans from following Europe. Fanon states, "This Europe where they are never done talking of man, yet murder men everywhere they find them, at the corner of everyone of their own streets, and in of all the corners of the globe."[48] Mazama, however, disagrees with Fanon's adoption of Marxism and stated that, "It may well be his espousal of Marxism that cause him to under estimate the devastating effect of conceptual incarceration and overall, belittle the role of culture in the struggle for freedom."[49]

The Negritude movement in France by the three proponents, Aime Cesaire, Leopold Sedar Senghor, and Leon Gontran Dumas, is analyzed by Mazama as having

---

[47] Ibid., 11.

[48] Fanon, *The Wretched of the Earth*, 235.

[49] Mazama, *The Afrocentric Paradigm*,15.

given Africans an appreciation of African culture. However, Senghor was still especially occupied with Europeans by his adoption of certain aspect of European culture. Senghor was captured by his allegiance to the French language. The fourth cornerstone in the conceptualization of Afrocentricity is the Kawaida theory by its creator, Maulana Karenga. The Kawaida theory states that the main problem of African people is the cultural crisis. The popular culture of African is unconscious and reactive towards life and its environment. However, a national culture is self-conscious collective thought and practice through which a people creates itself and introduces itself to history and humanity.[50]

Mazama states that "Diop major contribution was the making of the blackness of the ancient Egyptians into an scientific operational concept."[51] She explains that it was Hegel's influence on western thought that suggested Africa's lack of noticeable contributions to world history which made Diop's work so significant. Women's studies, an aspect of the Afrocentric paradigm, has developed in the discipline of Afro-American studies is the idea of women's studies. The main thrust of the Africana womanism theory was given by Clenora Hudson Weems.[52]

Weems coined the term Africana womanism and pointed out aspects of feminism that were inappropriate for black women. Firstly, feminism is fundamentally a European phenomenon, and it is based on European metaphysical principles. For example, there is

---

[50] Ibid., 19.

[51] Ibid., 20.

[52] Clenora Hudson Weems, *Africana Womanism, Afrocentric Paradigm*, 153-162.

a conflicting relationship between the genders where men are seen as the primary enemies of women. Secondly, feminism as it was developed in the 1880s, was blatantly racist. Hudson Weems argues that feminism does not and cannot reflect the beliefs or interests of African women. Based on Hudson Weems' philosophy, a focus on Afrocentricity is eminent.[53]

In his book, *African Centered Psychology*, Ajaniya Azibo Daudi includes an article that is described as "A General Paradigm of African Centered Social Work," a social struggle for the liberation of African people by Aminifu R. Harvey. This article is near in the usage of African culture and Africans in American culture as J. Baldwin's book on *African/Black Psychology*. The way Harvey treats black culture and how it can revitalize African consciousness in African Americans is similar to Baldwin's theories. In his introduction, Harvey lays out the central premise for African social work. Harvey states that, "Social Welfare can be defined as the process by which a group of people provides mechanism to ensure the well being of the members of their group. Group well being refers to groups' psychological emotional, physical, economic, social, and spiritual ability to enhance its existence as defined by the group members."[54]

Harvey suggests that to maximize a group opportunity for self-determination, the group's needs must match provisions of support in the environment. Therefore, knowledge about African civilization is a must and its need is apparent. Classical African civilization begins with the African history of African on the continent and the

---

[53] Ibid.

[54] Daudi, Ajaniya Azibo, Ed., *African Centered Psychology: A General Paradigm of African Centered Social Work*. Aminifu R. Harvey (Durham, NC: Carolina Academic Press, 2003), 109-129.

Diaspora before the invasions by Western Asians and Europeans. Africans were in the Western hemisphere long before they were brought here as kidnapped Africans according to Ivan Van Sertima.[55] Africans were trading with the indigenous people in what is now known as America and Africans influence those cultures. Proof of which are the many pyramids in the Americas. Researchers Latif and Latif provided documentation that African nations such as Mali, Songhay, Ethiopia, Nubia, and Kemet were old and had their golden age before Europeans developed any degree of civilization.[56]

The discovery of ancestors in Ethiopia dating back 4 million years was called the first family. L. S. B. Leakey's discovery of Lucy, a female found in Ethiopia dates back 4.5 million years ago. Scientists can trace the beginning of the human race in Africa from the foothills of the mountain of the moon near Lake Victoria and Mount Kilimanjaro. Many African scholars such as Cheikh Anta Diop, Josef Ben Jochannon, Jacob Carruthers and George James state that Kemet, or what Europeans called Egypt, provided the foundation for world civilization. Kemet, according to W. A. Budge's, *Egypt, the Light of the World*, had a written language and laid the foundation for humanistic existence based on belief in the spirituality of humans. Traditional African culture never separated the sacred from the secular.[57]

African culture focuses on the harmonious relationship between human beings and nature. The African philosophy was based on MAAT and is represented in the 42

---

[55] Ivan Van Sertima, *They Came Before Columbus: The African Presence in Ancient America*, (New York: Random House, 1977), 1-10.

[56] S. A. Latif and N. Latif, The African American Psychic Trauma (Chicago, IL: Latif Communications Group, Inc, 1994, 10.

[57] Ibid., 110.

confessions and or Declaration of Innocence (42 principles of MAAT). The Ancient

Kemetians employed the 42 principles as a guide for their moral behavior. Therefore,

there are foundations in African civilization for modern day social welfare and social

work carried out in the American context for which to build. Also, the modern ethnic

groups that exist in Africa carry the seeds from classical notions today. Diop has shown

this in his writings. This is the basis of civilization which began in the Nile Valley

cultures.

What reasons have caused Africans in the Diaspora and on the continent to be

unable to produce modern golden ages? The MAAFA, which is defined as the great

suffering, was African people enslavement in the West and their colonization on the

continent. Kwame Ture states that African continental development was halted by the

taking of 300 million African out of Africa by the most brutal means by European and

Arabs during the African slave trade. The effects of slavery are still within the African

mindscape. Joy Leury has called it post-traumatic slave syndrome; it still keeps the

African in the American trap with Anti-African behavior inherited from slavery.[58] Bobby

Wright stated that the indoctrination of Africans was mentacide which is the results of

oppression that causes the African to destroy other Africans. An example of mentacide is

the mis-education of Africans in the educational institutions that are set up in the United

States by white philanthropy. Mentacide compels mis-educated Africans to work toward

imitating Europeans and the betterment of Europeans American society at the expense of

their own self-interest. Also, the psychological paradox of internalization of the color

---

[58] Joy Leury, *Post-Traumatic Slave Syndrome*, (Milwaukee: Uptone Press, 2005), 14.

paradox creates class problems for Africans. The skin color complex, both the conscious and unconscious, affect the mental health of Africans on the continent and in the Diaspora.[59] The fact that blacks worship a white Jesus in Christianity is a sign of mis-orientation. All people usually set up religion as it reflects their own image, thus Africans still suffer spiritual slavery by worshipping white gods and white saviors. For many people, Africans' self-worth is determined by material possession and the power to obtain these possessions even at the cost of someone else's life or their own.

How can Africans change their condition of dependence on Europeans in America? Self determination is a social work value and an African principle of the Nguzo Saba. It is the real force behind the African's drive in the liberation of African people from psychological and environmental slavery.[60] Self-determination is defined as Africans defining who they are, and their ability to name and speak for themselves. The seven principles of Nguzo Saba can be used to liberate African dependence on foreign values such as materialism. Afrocentric models of social work are represented by African social welfare programs.

Harvey, in Azibo's book, gives three models of African centered social welfare programs. Firstly, the Progressive Life Center is a private nonprofit community based agency that strives to improve mental health services through culturally competent therapeutic techniques. The second model is a comprehensive family preservation treatment program for addicted African-American women that include treatment

---

[59] Bobby Wright, "Mentacide: The Ultimate Threat to the Black Race," unpublished manuscript.

[60] Ibid., 118.

approaches drawn from traditional African culture. A third model is comprehensive

African centered programs for African adolescent males and their families developed and

implemented at the MAAT Center, a community based nonprofit agency.[61] Information

on the leader of the Shrine of the Black Madonna (Reverend Albert Cleage) follows in

Chapter III. Reverend Cleage is a good example of Afrocentric personality in action and

practice.

---

[61] Ibid., 123.

CHAPTER III

HISTORICAL BACKGROUND

Jaramogi Abebe Agyeman, also known as Albert B. Cleage, Jr., was born on June 13, 1911 in Detroit, Michigan, and died on February 20, 2000 on the Beulah Land Farm in South Carolina. An ordained minister, Reverend Cleage was the eldest of seven children born to Dr. Albert I. Buford Cleage, Sr. and Pearl Reed Cleage. According to his mother, Pearl Reed Cleage, Albert Cleage did not have a safe little dream but a big dream. His dream was to restore black people to their original place of power and dignity in the world.[1]

Reverend Cleage served as a minister to a number of churches before he founded The Shrine of the Black Madonna, the premier Black Nationalist Church in America. The Shrine, as it is affectionately called by community members of the Historic West End District in Atlanta, Georgia, is a part of the Pan African Orthodox Christian Church (PAOCC). Reverend Cleage understood that young people were the revolutionary element in the church. He believed that the youth could translate the radical message of Jesus into action and carry the church to the "next level." This "next level" involved encouraging the church to make political, social, and economic issues a part of the church's mission.[2]

---

[1] Sis Carolyn Dara Starkey and M. W. William, *Diallo Brown Jubilee Souvenir Booklet*, Detroit Michigan. 2003.

[2] Ibid., 29.

Reverend Cleage began his career by participating in the St. Cyprian Episcopal Church Youth Group while a student at North Western High School in Detroit, Michigan. Later, while in college at Wayne State University, he became the unofficial youth pastor at the Plymouth Congressional Church and was also the Director of the Plymouth Youth League. Reverend Cleage's father was what was known as a *race man* and inspired his son to become a community activist. His mother was also active in the community working with the local school board in a campaign to increase the number of black teachers hired.[3]

As the young Reverend Cleage began exploring his life's calling, he became a social worker, assisting families and children. One year later in 1938, he enrolled at Oberlin Graduate School of Theology in Oberlin, Ohio. He studied hard and upon graduation, became acting Minister of The Church for the Fellowship of All People in 1943. The Church for the Fellowship of All People was an integrated church, which was rare during this time period in American history. The Chandler Memorial Congregational Church in Lexington, Kentucky was the next stop for Reverend Cleage on his journey toward a church with a more intentional African orientation.[4]

In 1944, Reverend Cleage attended the University of Southern California in Los Angeles, California. While taking ministerial classes, he also studied cinematography. Reverend Cleage abandoned his academic career shortly before completing his Ph.D. to

---

[3] Ibid., 30.

[4] Ibid.

assume another pastorate.[5] In 1945, Reverend Cleage became pastor of the St. John's

Congregational Church in Springfield, Massachusetts, one of the most prestigious black

churches in New England. He served as Youth Minister and his focus was fighting the

status quo by combating police brutality in black communities. While at St. John's, he

also developed a youth athletic program. His basketball program produced some of the

state's top basketball players.

In addition to his growing ministerial responsibilities, Reverend Cleage was

chairman of the local National Association for the Advancement of Colored People

(NAACP) Housing Committee. He was tireless in his efforts to help people obtain

decent housing and was involved in one high profile conflict over some property owned

by the popular black minister, Dr. William Deberry. Reverend Cleage's church won a

settlement for $11,000 to buy a number of properties. He left St. John's in 1950 to

become pastor of St. Mark's Presbyterian Church in Detroit where his father was on the

Board of Trustees.[6]

In 1952, Reverend Cleage was chosen to head the NAACP Membership

Committee in Detroit. He was successful in making it the most affluent and powerful

chapter in the country. As a result of his hard work, Reverend Cleage was elected to the

Executive Board for the Detroit Chapter of the NAACP. In the meantime, by advocating

a new and more community-based direction for St. Mark's, he incurred the wrath of the

Board of Trustees and was dismissed from his pastorship. Defiantly, he spoke on the

---

[5] Ibid., 31.

[6] Ibid.

following Sunday to the church and delivered a very critical sermon, the core of which emphasized the need for a new kind of church. More than 300 members walked out behind him as he finished his final sermon. Reverend Cleage, along with his loyal followers, established the St. Mark's Congregational Church.[7] The church was later renamed the Central Congregational Church. In 1954, the church bought a sixteen-room mansion on Chicago Boulevard in Detroit. This house became a thriving combination of church and community life. When the nearby Brewster Pilgrim Congressional Church decided to sell its church, Reverend Cleage's church raised the money to purchase it. It was through persistence and focus of the members and the vision that this monetary goal was realized.

Malcolm X was a dynamic minister during the same era and shared many of the Black Nationalist viewpoints of Reverend Cleage. Indeed, they often spoke at some of the same black political rallies in and around Detroit. They became friends as well as political allies. Malcolm X admired the political savvy and business acumen of Rev. Cleage so much that he offered Reverend Cleage a position as lead Minister of a Muslim Mosque in Detroit, but Reverend Cleage respectfully declined, telling the Minister he was a committed Christian.[8]

While serving as president of a junior high school's Parent Teacher Association (PTA) from 1962 through 1969, Reverend Cleage helped reshape the Detroit Public School system. The PTA advocated having a Black Studies Program throughout the

---

[7] Ibid., 32.

[8] Ibid., 38.

system and filed a lawsuit in court. Again, Reverend Cleage worked tirelessly until the

suit was won. As a result of his efforts, according to Sis. Carolyn Dara Starkey, he

brought a new level of community control to the education process. [9]

The Cleage family established the *Illustrated News*, a weekly newspaper

distributed by the church members; circulation reached its height when they distributed

more than 65,000 newspapers. The *Illustrated News* proved to be an important tool in

reshaping the views of Detroit's black community during the turbulent 1960s. Reverend

Cleage, through the influence and advocacy of this community vehicle, helped to create

job opportunities for blacks at companies such as Sears, Chrysler, Tip Top Bread, and A

& P Grocery Stores.[10] At this point in time, Reverend Cleage began to crystallize his

own particular religious beliefs relative to the challenges that black people faced in

American society.

The book, *Black Theology: a Documentary History* by black theologians James

Cone and Gayroud Wilmore substantiates that Reverend Cleage first coined the term

"Black Theology." Under Cleage's leadership, Central Congregational Church was

evolving from what had begun as a Christian outreach church to what became a vehicle

to empower the black community.[11] Reverend Cleage observed the worldwide quest for

black power in the liberation struggles of Liberians and other people in Africa. He was

aware of the civil rights struggle in America. When Cleage synthesized all of his

---

[9] Ibid., 39.

[10] Ibid.

[11] Ibid.

experiences and observations, he then decided that Black Nationalism was a necessary key for unlocking black liberation throughout the world. This was a controversial position in the 1960s because the goal of integration was considered sacred and was viewed as the primary goal of the black struggles.[12]

The Civil Rights March in July of 1963 in Detroit, Michigan was a testament to Reverend Cleage's wide ranging influence. During an important meeting of the NAACP, a banquet was held in honor of Reverend Cleage. On this occasion, he announced a plan for a civil rights march downtown which was to travel down Woodward Avenue, and the main artery would culminate at Cobo Hall, a huge convention center in Detroit. His audience was informed that Reverend Martin Luther King, Jr. would also be in attendance. Reverend Cleage's speech galvanized the audience and planning for the event began soon thereafter. He established an organization to facilitate the logistical challenge associated with the planning of such a large march and called the Detroit Council of Human Relations to organize the march.[13] The organization anticipated a crowd of 100,000. The day of this Freedom March over 300,000 people attended. Reverend Cleage gave a fiery speech that almost caused a riot, but he skillfully controlled and excited the crowd.

When the Detroit Council of Human Relations moved to its next project, they formed the Northern Christian Leadership Conference (NCLC). Reverend Cleage called for radical leadership and would challenge the moderate solo of King. However,

---

[12] Ibid.

[13] Ibid., 40.

Reverend Cleage met hard resistance, and Reverend C. L. Franklin called for the ousting

of the Nationalist faction. Cleage called for a press conference where he resigned from

his office as Chairman of the Detroit Council of Human Relations. He then called for a

grass roots conference on Black Nationalism with Malcolm X as the keynote speaker.

Malcolm X made his legendary speech "Message to the Grassroots" at that rally.[14]

In 1963, Reverend Cleage, along with other leaders, launched the Freedom NOW

Party. Under this party's banner Reverend Cleage became the first black man since

Reconstruction to run for governor of a state and meet the challenge posed by an often

lethargic black voting block. Cleage organized the black community around the concept

of planking or leveraging votes by only voting for a select few candidates in a multi-seat

election such as city council. The strategy yielded the *three plus one campaign* and the

four and no more campaign. This strategy was responsible for gaining great power and

control for blacks in city governance and politics. The use of a successful proactive

political strategy led to the popular black slate, a political manifesto designed to advance

black power in inner city Detroit. Also, this helped the election of Coleman Young as the

mayor of Detroit.[15]

Eventually, Reverend Cleage created the Inner City Organizing Committee

(ICOC), which gave the community control and development. There were numerous

satellite organizations, such as the Inner City Housing Conference, the Black Retail

Employees Association, and the Black Teachers Workshop. There were Black Christian

---

[14] Ibid., 41.

[15] Ibid.

Nationalist (BCN) conventions that eventually led to a nationwide organization. In January of 1972, the church purchased the National Training Center. This was the Outreach Ministry of the Pan African Orthodox Christian Church and its acquisition signaled a new evolutionary phase, i.e. completely independent, economic self-sufficiency and political self-interest, as a means of building power within the community.

Cleage argued that the church should be at the center of this transformation. He later stressed the need for nation building. This new phase of black national status fervor brought an end of the public ministry of the spiritual and political journey of Rev. Albert Cleage. After 1972 until his passing, that is his dance with the ancestors on February 20, 2000, Jaramogi struggled to build a new church and direct the Shrine as a national organization. These organizations have made great contributions to the liberation struggles of black people in America. Today, the Shrine has a church in Houston, Texas; Atlanta, Georgia; and Detroit, Michigan. It also purchased 5,000 acres of land called Beulah Land, located in South Carolina. The Shrine's latest work has been the establishment of Black Holocaust Museums. After the Detroit Rebellion of 1967, Reverend Cleage organized the City-Wide Citizen's Action Committee (CCAC) to rebuild the city starting with the Black Star Co-op Market, a grocery store, Black Star Co-op Housing, and the Black Star Service Center and Gas Station. He also created The Shrine of the Black Madonna Bookstore and Cultural Center.[16]

---

[16] Ibid., 42.

Reverend Cleage wrote two books: *The Black Messiah* and *Black Christian Nationalism: New Direction for the Black Church.* These two books became very popular and were used as training tools for young Black Christian Nationalists. He was convinced that the black church was the only institution that could build independent power for black people.[17]

Reverend Albert B. Cleage, Jr. (Jaramogi Abebegyeman) and His Philosophy of Liberation

God is constantly expanding a unified cosmic energy field, combining the four fundamentals forces of nature in which we live, move, and have our being and from which we derive life meanings, values, and direction. We conceive a God as the cosmic power and creative intelligence out of which all things are created. We experience God in our worship in our communal fellowship and most completely in the theosophical experience of Kugasana. The chasm that separates us from God is our own selfishness and individualism, which makes us more concerned about our individual salvation than we are about the liberation of all black people.[18]

The African Origin of Christianity Historically

Christianity is a black man's religion created out of the experience of black people in Africa. A black man in America can follow any of the historic religions of the world. He can also be confident that he worshiped as his forefathers did at some time in the black man's past.[19]

---

[17] Ibid., 43.

[18]. The National Recommitment—Sunday Commemorative Booklet, June 14, 1998, The Shrine of the Black Madonna, 8.

[19] Ibid., 9.

The Shrine of the Black Madonna

"The church is a community of persons existing in a unified energy field which is

God, voluntarily associated together because they share a common commitment to this

supreme power out of which they have been created and upon which they depend for the

incarnate life force which is human life."[20]

> The church, as a transforming community, mediates the power of God. The church acts for God in the world. Those things which we have come to expect from God—comfort, solace, healing, security, guidance, help, forgiveness, strength, understanding, purpose, and an after life—must be delivered by the communal fellowship of the church through which God has elected to act because we are the chosen and have established a covenant relationship. God as cosmic energy and creative intelligence has no other body to house the infinite power of the unified field through which all possibilities are open to the church.[21]

Reverend Cleage on Commitment

> Black Christian Nationalism is a movement and we demanded serious commitment as Jesus the Black Messiah demanded serious commitment when he called his disciples. He expected men to leave everything to come and follow him with complete loyalty, discipline, and devotion to the liberation of black people. We believe that nothing is more sacred than the liberation of black people.
>
> Jesus was a Black Messiah, the son of a black woman, a son of the Black Nation Israel. The historical and anthropological evidence abound to prove the blackness of Jesus, so let us not waste time whipping a dead horse (or a nonexistent white messiah). As important as the fact that Israel and Jesus were black is the fact that Jesus was a revolutionary leader engaged in a liberation struggle against the white gentile world. In light of these facts, the meaning of the Bible is dramatically changed and Christianity is a black man's religion relevant to the black revolution. The black church must build on this foundation.[22]
>
> Black Christian Nationalism is a movement and we use the science of KUA. The practice of KUA offers complete therapy for the awakened group, utilizing meditation, movements, sacraments, and rituals to provide a complete system of body mind training; designed to lead the group to that mystical spiritual

---

[20] Ibid.. 8.

[21] Ibid., 9.

[22] Ibid.

opening which permits the incarnate life force to be touched by the cosmic energy and the creative intelligence of the unified cosmic energy field, which is God. The group is healed by the Kugsanna experience of God and receives the power to heal others and bring the world, its government and institutions into conformity with the Will of God.[23]

Revolutionary Love

There are three components of Revolutionary Love:

1. **There must be compassion on the part of one for another**. People are not perfect, they don't always do what they should but when they sin (violate the law) you should confront them. If they are truly sorry for their sins, then you should forgive them.

2. **There must be service**. You must give totally of yourself to the accomplishment of goals that transcend your selfishness and serve the interest of the group of which you are a part. Service demands that we sacrifice and invest all that we have in the movement.

3. **There must be a constant awareness of reality**. Once you understand the nature of our social condition as a people, your need for other people becomes obvious. When you realize that you need other people, you will become more conscious of how you treat them.[24]

The Reality of the Cosmos

Everything in the universe is energy (matter is compressed energy). We are created by God out of the very substance of divinity. The spark of divinity in each of us is the life force. Through KUA we are able to re-align and re-activate the energy in ourselves, thereby healing by restoring the harmonious relationship with the cosmic as intended by God.[25]

---

[23] Ibid.

[24] Ibid., 14.

[25] Ibid.

Reverend Cleage on Survival

> We will survive. We have lived in a dream world of fantasy which threatened to engulf and destroy us. A mighty giant awakening from a deep sleep, we stretch, rub the sleep from our eyes, look at the world and what it has done to us and cry out in rage. We are not afraid. Without jobs, money or skills, we will survive the anguish of our suffering, created out of the very substance of God; we have come together in the transforming community where the power of God is. We labor in love and communal fellowship to build a promised land. We are destined to inherit the earth. So, stand tall, be conscious of the divinity within you. Be proud of what we are, be proud of what we can become and thank God who made us the most beautiful people and the best of people. Black is beautiful, black is strong, and black is good. The secret of our beauty, strength and goodness lies in our loyalty and total submission to the will of God. Kuyitoa—We Will Survive.[26]

The History of the Shrine of the Black Madonna

Member of the Pan-African Orthodox Christian Church.

The Shrine of the Black Madonna was founded in 1953 when 300 members of a Detroit Presbyterian Church, led by the late Reverend Albert B. Cleage, Jr., abandoned the church over a question of church involvement in community affairs. The members adopted the name St. Mark's Congregational Church and began holding worship services at the Crossman School on Clairmont Street in Detroit. The church changed its name in 1954 from St. Mark's Congregational Church to Central Congregational Church and purchased its first piece of property in 1954, which was a mansion located at 2254 Chevy Boulevard in Detroit, Michigan. The structure was used as a parsonage and was the center of all of the church's activities, excluding the morning worship.

The property the church purchased was the Brewster-Pilgrim Congregational Church at 7625 Linwood Street in Detroit in 1957. This is presently the location of the

---

[26] Tenth Anniversary of Shrine #10, National Tribute to Jaramogi Abebe Agyeman, June 1987, 19.

Shrine of the Black Madonna #1. The Shrine membership doubled between 1957 and 1958. In 1957, Reverend Cleage led a successful political campaign to save the 13th Congressional District from redistricting.[27] The politics also involved education. The first fight against the Detroit school system was launched in 1962, and the first issue of the organization's publication, the *Illustrated News* was released to a circulation of 35,000. Reverend Cleage spoke at the 1963 Freedom March in Detroit before Dr. Martin Luther King took the stage to deliver his famous "I Have a Dream" speech.

Reverend Cleage and Malcolm X spoke at the Grassroots Conference in Detroit in 1963 in which Malcolm X encouraged participants of the conference to join The Shrine of the Black Madonna. The church organized the first all Black political party, called the Freedom Now Party in which Reverend Cleage was elected leader.[28] In 1964, Cleage became the first black man to run for governor of the State of Michigan since Reconstruction. The party then possessed several political action groups from the Inner City Organizing Committee, founded in 1966, including: the Black Retail Employees Association, the Inner City Parents Council, the Black Teacher Workshop, the Inner City Students Organization, the Afro-American Committee against the Racist Wars, and the Michigan Inner City Organizing Committee.

The church's membership grew tremendously during the late 1960s and throughout the 1970s. The church's focus, structure, and sensitivity to young black revolutionaries of the highly charged Black Power Movement provided solace to this

---

[27] Jubilee Souvenir Booklet, advisor Jaramogi Menelik Kimathi, Editor-in-Chief Sister Carolyn Dara Starkey, 48.

[28] Ibid., 49.

group while other churches shunned them. In March 1967, the church launched the Black Christian Nationalist Movement. The movement reflected the church's belief that Jesus was a Black Messiah. *The Black Messiah*, a collection of explosive sermons by Cleage was published in 1968.

In 1969, the concept of a Black Nation within a Nation began to evolve. The Black Christian Manifesto outlined the Church's effort to restructure the rituals, organizations and programs of the Black Church as a Black Nation. In 1970, the Church officially changed its name to The Shrine of the Black Madonna and opened a bookstore and cultural center on Livernois Street in Detroit, Michigan. The African naming ceremonies and the new holy days were adopted, and a food co-op program was established. The Liberation Triangle was developed and moral or ethical guidelines for membership were established. The University of Michigan and Western Michigan University College cadres were formed in 1971.[29]

The Shrine of the Black Madonna #3 was established in Northwest Detroit in 1972. The Atlanta College cadre and the Flint Michigan College cadre were formed in 1973. The Black Slate, an advocacy and political action organization was also formed in 1973 in Detroit, Michigan. The Black Slate was instrumental in the election of Detroit's first black mayor, Coleman Young. It was also involved with the elections of mayors Andrew Young, Maynard Jackson, and Shirley Franklin in Atlanta, Georgia. In Chicago, Illinois, The Black Slate influenced the election of Mayor Harold Washington, and in local areas and a number of states such as Georgia, Michigan, and Texas.

---

[29] Ibid.

The Shrine of the Black Madonna #2 was established on the east side of Detroit in 1974. Its first service was a memorial to Malcolm X. The official opening of Atlanta's Shrine #9 was held in Atlanta, GA in 1975. The Kalamazoo Expansion Cadre opened Shrine #7 in Houston, Texas in 1977.

The first Pan-African Synod was held in Houston, Texas. Black Christian Nationalist Church, was replaced with Pan-African Orthodox Christian Church in 1978. The name draws upon the Marcus Garvey's African Orthodox Church's theology. The church's constitution bestowed the title of First-Holy Patriarch on Cleage.[30]

The first KUA Meditation and Educational center (Shrine #5) and the Technological Center (Shrine #4) opened in Detroit in 1979. In 1981, Mtoto House, a Kibbutz-like early learning and living program was founded in Houston, Texas. The Beulah Land Farm Project was founded in 1981. The project's goal of BeulahLand was to raise funds to acquire a fully independent 5,000 acre farm to be used for adult and youth skill training, to provide quality whole foods for members, to serve as a retreat for youth, and to provide jobs for members of the church.[31]

A multi-million dollar African Cultural Complex was opened in 1986 at Shrine #10 in Houston, Texas. The first Black Holocaust exhibit opened at the Cultural Center in Atlanta, Georgia under the tutelage of Reverend Velma Maia Thomas, depicting the horrors of the enslavement process. The subsequent exhibits also were installed in Detroit and Houston. The 1999 opening of Beulah Land Farm signaled the beginning of

---

[30] Ibid., 50.

[31] Ibid.

a new era. The farm was located in Abbeville, South Carolina and is still functioning today. The farm includes cattle, poultry, and a catfish operation.[32]

In February of 2000, the founder and Holy Patriarch Jaramogi Abebe Agyeman, Reverend Albert B. Cleage, died at Beulah Land Farm. Thousands attended his memorial service. Among the people who delivered remarks at the service were Haki Madhubuti, Susan Taylor, Carolyn Cheeks Kilpatrick, and his daughter Pearl Cleage. Demosthene Nelson, the 2nd Holy Patriarch of the Church, succeeded him. He is also known as Jaramogi Menelik Kimathi. He holds a Master of Divinity from Yale and is the author of the Nursery Kua System for spiritual and intellectual development of pre-school youth.[33]

In January 2002, the Akwaabu Community Center began operation in Detroit, Michigan. The center offers computer training, after school programs, youth and adult Bible classes and African history classes. It also provides low cost office and meeting space for community groups. On August 1-3, 2003, the Church celebrated its Golden 50th Anniversary Jubilee.

---

[32] Ibid., 51.

[33] Ibid., 52-53.

CHAPTER IV

FINDINGS

Observation/Participant

Cultural Center, Shrine of the Black Madonna, Atlanta, GA

The researcher observed the Holocaust Museum at the Shrine of the Black Madonna from August 2009 to September 2009. The Holocaust Museum features pictures and writings about Harriett Tubman, Sojourner Truth, Dred Scott and other historical figures. There is a framed picture of a slave who had scars from beatings on his back by a white master. Also, the researcher observed a mannequin of a man with dripping blood and a rope around his neck. There are pictures of chained Africans and their shackles. The Africans are shown tightly packed in under the deck of a ship. Africans are shown in the cotton fields on the plantation. State petitions for freedom are in the museum. Artifacts from the slave era consisting of chains and shackles are shown with sample cotton. There is a box shown at the museum that illustrates the amount of space each African had aboard the ships during the middle passage. There are also artifacts from the slavery and Jim Crow periods.

The museum has candles and a sign-in sheet to record each visitor and to acknowledge their ancestors who endured the MAAFA of Africans captured in Africa and enslaved in the New World. The Cultural Center has a collection of books by African authors and African artwork from the homeland for sale. Afrocentric candles are also on display for sale.

Beulah Land Farms, South Carolina

Beulah Land is 4,000 acres of land bought by the Shrine (see Figure 1). This land was undeveloped at the time of purchase. Since that period, the Shrine members have constructed roads, houses, fish ponds, and a chapel. The members have constructed housing facilities for visiting members. The Shrine has purchased cattle, chickens, hogs or pigs and horses for the farm.

Figure 2. Beulah Land Farms

The researcher visited and toured the farm in August 2009 and photographed different sites at the farm. The researcher met the head minister and people who live on the farm. He also watched a video of members who were doing work on the farm.

History Class: June 2009 – January 31, 2010

The researcher has attended history classes at the Shrine since June 2009. The

history class is held at the Shrine on Saturdays in the Founders Hall. The history class is

named the African University. The subject discussed is African history from the

beginning of man to the present. There is a video library in the Founders Hall that has a

collection of video history of Africa. There are over 1,000 videos of African history and

culture. In August 2009 at the Hall, the researcher witnessed a naming ceremony. The

neophyte was given an African name. The neophyte had to read certain books on African

history. The final ceremony features the neophyte receiving a spear and a new African

name.

The history classes always begin with a libation ceremony where the ancestors are

invited to join the class. The members call the name of known and unknown ancestors.

These ancestors have set examples of wisdom, courage, and sacrifice for the existence of

Africans through time eternal. They are remembered for how they fought and died for

the continuation of African culture and life. The pouring of libation is an African

tradition.

African history is taught by a shrine mwalimu and minister. The class has

featured numerous African scholars who give guest lectures to the class. The African

history, taught since June 2009, includes the following topics:

A.   The Early History of Man

B.   The Nile Valley Civilization
     1. Ethopia

      2. Nubia
      3. Kemit (Egypt)

C. The Central African Empires
      1. Monopotopa
      2. Zimbabwe
      3. Congo

D. West African Empires
      1.   Ghana
      2.   Mali
      3.   Songhay

E. Slave Trade in Africa
      1. Muslim Slavery
      2. White Christian Slavery
        (a) Europe
        (b) Middle East

F. The African Presence in the World
      1. Europe
      2. The Americas
      3. Asia

G. The Slave Revolts
      1. Haiti
      2. USA (250 Revolts)
      3. South America
      4. Caribbean
      5. U.S. Civil War

H. History of Africans in the U.S.A.
      1. Africans in the U.S.A.'s Slavery Period
      2. Reconstruction
      3. Jim Crow
      4. Harlem Renaissance
      5. Civil Rights Era
      6. The Black Power Era
      7. Post-Black Power to the Present

I. Colonialism in Africa
      1. The Colonial Wars
      2. Independence

    3. Modern Independence and Post Colonial Wars
    4. Angola
    5. Namibia
    6. Zimbabwe
    7. South Africa
    8. Kenya
    9. Tanzania
    10. Other States

J.   Modern Civil Wars
    1. Angola
    2. Congo
    3. Namibia
    4. Sierra Leone
    5. Liberia
    6. Rwanda
    7. Darfur

K.   Student Lectures
    1. Jews and Black (Ankh)
    2. Mysteries (Modog)
    3. Haitian Revolution (Leon Davis)
    4. Seasoning (Sister Oni Oluremi)

Worship Service and Community Action—August 2009 – January 2010: Order of Service

- Call to Worship – Candle lighting ritual and music by the band begin the service.

- Black National Anthem "Lift Every Voice and Sing" – The band performs music.

- Praise and Worship – Words of Inspiration by the lead minister and music is performed.

- Alter Prayer/Call – Everyone is called to the Altar. Scripture lesson – Words of Wisdom from the Bible. The worship service is composed of a responsive reading and meditation - speaker and audience call and response.

- Communion (The four principles of communion with God are recited): (1) KutaFuta, (2) FutaMunga, (3) Kuga Sana, and (4) Kujitoa

- Chant four principles.

- Song and Music – Choir and band perform songs and other music.

- Sermon – Minister or Pastor

- Invitational Hymn Songs and Call to Join

- Offering/Hymn

- The choir sings the hymn, "Rise Nation Rise, One Nation, One Race, One Destiny"

- The worship service is followed by Communion of Church and Socializing with guests and members.

Community Action

Community Dinners
1. Breakfast
2. Group Dinners
3. Special Days
   a. Community Festivals (May)
   b. Malcolm X Day (May)
   c. Marcus Garvey Day (August)
   d. African Liberation Day (May)
   e. Kwanzaa Nguzo Saba (December-January)
   f. Special Lecture Series
   g. Special Events
4. Dinners
5. Dances (African)
6. Trips (Africa and Diaspora)
7. Church Schools
   a. Elementary
   b. Workshops for College Students
   c. Rites of Passage
   d. Wednesday Lectures
   e. Homeless Meals Outreach-Bishop Aboutsi

Qualitative Findings

Research Questions

Research Question 1: How does the Shrine of the Black Madonna create Afrocentric personalities in its members?

Research Question 2: How will members of the Shrine using communal economics, self-knowledge and an African orientation reflect the collective identity of the African saying, I am because we are, because we are, therefore I Am?

The interviews were conducted by the researcher with ten respondents who are the leaders of the Shrine in Atlanta and interpreted from the perspective of Afrocentricity. The five categories that were used to record the findings of this study are as follows: African Culture, Black Liberation Theology, Black Nationalism, Transformation, and Communalism.

African Culture

The interviews provided the data for the findings by using the seven categories to record the responses of those ten elite members. The first category is African Culture. The Nguzo Saba created by Maulana Karenga was adopted from African Culture. The seven principles are: (1) Imoja (Unity); (2) Kujichagulia (Self-determination); (3) Ujimma (Collective Work and Responsibility); (4) Ujamaa (Cooperative Economics); (5) Nia (Purpose); (6) Kuumba (Creativity); and (7) Imani (Faith).

Respondent Mwalimu Diallo on African Culture: Unity—the first questions of Mwalimu on the vision of the Shrine by way of his` position. "My vision is that we are building a better world for black people and liberating black people. This position has aided me in building a better world for Black people."[1]

The next Nguzo Saba principle of self-determination is reflected in the following responses of Mwalimu Diallo to inquiries. "God does not want us to be slaves; we can be empowered through the power of God. All things are possible with God. We have the right to have self-determination and this is a God given right. God will give us the strength to change our conditions."[2] In terms of collective economics, Beulah Land could not have come into being without the collective efforts of everyone in the church.[3] This is the principle of cooperative economics.

The Nguzo Saba principles of Ujamaa are reflected in Mwalimu Diallo statement. "It is unfortunate that in this day that a lot of folks do not feel the need for us to pool our resources but it is even more critical today than then. The reason we suffer today is because we do not pool our resources. We provide jobs and opportunities for other people, other races rather than pooling our resources for ourselves"[4]

The principle of Imani, faith, is reflected in the responses of Mwalimu Diallo's statement. "With faith, we can do all things. One of the biggest challenges that we have

---

[1] Mwalimu Diallo, Interview by Leon W. Davis, tape recording, The Shrine of the Black Madonna, Atlanta, GA, 8 August 2009.

[2] Ibid.

[3] Ibid.

[4] Ibid.

as a people is to believe in ourselves, if we believe in God and believe in God's power in us, we can do anything"[5]

The next respondent was Jaribu Chitundu, Worship Minister and choir member. The Nguzo Saba principle Ujima is reflected in Jaribu's statement. Collective work and responsibility is stated as, "Whether assisting in group meetings or interacting with one another on a daily basis. It teaches us how to work together and how to give constructive criticism when necessary and where we have the opportunities to correct one another and to hold people to the standard of being a Black Christian Nationalist."[6]

The principle of self-determination is reflected in Jaribu's statement "to be self sufficient, to know who you are as black person living in America to create institutions that serve, the purpose of uplifting and restoring slave black people through Black Christian Nationalism, that we are to be self sufficient ourselves and to build institutions that serve our interest and uplift us to restore our human possibilities"[7] The research statement, "I am because we are, we are therefore I am" is reflected here by Jaribu: "You have the values of forgiveness, because you can have the Christian values of forgiveness or going the extra mile, there is no nation building without this. If you do not include that 'I am my brother's keeper or I am because we are, there is no nation building.'"[8] The Nguzo Saba principle of Ujima and Ujamaa are reflected in Jaribu's statement as follows:

---

[5] Ibid.

[6] Jaribu Chitundu, Interviewed by Leon W. Davis tape recording, The Shrine of the Black Madonna, Atlanta, GA 8 August 2009.

[7] Ibid.

[8] Ibid.

"Our director taught us that the Nguzo Saba principles are embedded in the theology of the church or shrine. We have the principles of communal work, working together to sustain our own institutions."[9]

The next respondent is Cardinal Jabari Henry, Chief Administrator of the Shrine. The Nguzo Saba principle of Umoja is reflected in this statement by Cardinal Jabari, "When we have the book store in Detroit, Atlanta and Houston, it is that Umoja unity that we all want, when you see the Shrine in Houston, you see a bookstore, in Atlanta you see one, we are trying to do all the same thing. Therefore, this is the Umoja element of the Nguzo Saba."[10] Cardinal Jabri is reflecting on the cultural center that is present at the three regions of the Shrine.

The principles of Ujima and Ujamaa are reflected in Jabari's statement on the Nguzo Saba principles used by the Shrine. "Identification or collective work and responsibility or Ujima, cooperative economics, a book store is the good example, where everyone can come in and purchase a book that will give them some self worth or self esteem about themselves. We do this from a nonprofit point of view, we are not trying to get a profit from it. The project is a unselfish cooperative economic element is there, nobody gets rich."[11] Also, we have 4,000 acres of farm land in Beulah Land. Beulah Land is an expression of our giving without seeing but believing that we as a group and region can put together a kind of economic plan that would allow us to purchase four

---

[9] Jabari Henry, Interviewed by Leon W. Davis, tape recording at 667 Peeples Street, Atlanta, GA,13 March 2009, 14.

[10] Ibid.

[11] Ibid.

thousand acres in 2000. We gave enormous amounts of monies to this and so we could

have land that we could grow food and have fish, cows, and timber to benefit our

people."[12] African culture is expressed in this statement by Jabari. "We in the Shrine

recognize the person gift that they bring to the benefit of the group. Traditionally, our

ancestors, when a person was born, there was a ritual with the elders or the doctors of that

ritual that would ask the basic questions, what gift does this person bring to the group, to

the tribe or community. We are trying to carry on that same philosophy today."[13]

Next Mwalimu Olatunji explains African Culture through cooperative economics

and the Nguzo Saba.

> For us to achieve our ultimate goal of nation building or liberation, controlling our
> own economic, political, social destines and realities, we understand that clearly
> that a free people have to have the ability to feed themselves. Rather than waiting
> for a handout from our oppressor and depending on his institution to feed us,
> therefore we have pooled our resources together and purchase land of our own.
> This is where we can grow our own food, feed ourselves as a people, and continue
> to feed the black nation.[14]

Cardinal Mwende Brown, CEO and Pastor of the Shrine of the Black Madonna of

Atlanta, explains African culture found in the Nguzo Saba principles of cooperative

economics, Ujima and Ujamaa. He states "Beulah Land is for the community. However,

we are in our tenth year of having Beulah Land. We are in its early development stages.

When you look at Beulah Land as a process or as an idea, Beulah land in South Carolina,

it is a portable concept which can take place in any urban city where you have some land.

---

[12] Ibid.

[13] Mwalimu Olatunja Cotton, Interviewed by Leon E. Davis tape recording, The Shrine of the Black Madonna, Atlanta, GA 15 March 2009.

[14] Ibid.

You can cultivate the land. People can invest in the land, their time and resources, where you can reap the harvest of the land. You can employ people on one hand, also it can service the people which is a greater importance."[15] Cardinal Mwende Brown also talks about how the Shrine deals with capitalism in the society it is living within.

> It is a concept of collective economics, Beulah Land, where you do have capitalism as an economic system but you can also have something to counter it, communalism. Therefore, it is an exchange or money can be generated, it is a collective; this collective economy allows one to do for a greater number of people.[16]

Cardinal Mwende explains, "Money goes into the community pocket, therefore you have a process where I work on a farm also, I am part of your community and from the farm it allows a school to be built. Those people that work inside the network can build living quarters also."[17] He also explains how Beulah Land comes to influence other people within the nation.

> The more people you have inside the church's orbit the more people you can take care of and you do not make as much money as other capitalist companies, but the children in your community are properly educated. The people have housing and the elderly are housed. It is the economics that is generated from Beulah Land that allows for more things to be done and have an impact on people outside the church because they are part of the orbit the Shrine functions in.[18]

---

[15] Mwende Brown, Interviewed by Leon W. Davis tape recording, The Shrine of the Black Madonna, 12 March 2009.

[16] Ibid.

[17] Ibid.

[18] Ibid.

Cardinal Mwende on the Nguzo Saba concepts: "The Nguzo Saba principles, Umoja,

Unite, purpose, Ujima, provide an alternative for blacks in this society.[19]

Ifetayo Jaha Tumpe is a group leader and societal leader of the Shrine. She states:

"Well for one, Beulah Land farms is 4000 acres, it is beautiful and the times I have gone

there, one sees fish, cattle, horses, chickens, and goats. We have gone to Beulah Land to

help repair buildings, do farming, and enjoy the fresh scenery. They have plans for other

kinds of things, lumber, water, and fish. This is a perfect example of how you can pool

your resources and be powerful."[20]

Sundiata Lane, Chief of Security; shared his comments before the Nguzo Saba

symbols became mainstream. He articulates, "It was bringing people together through

communal work and communal finances, these principles are the tools of the Nguzo

Saba."[21] Cardinal Hodari Omari, who is the Assistant Chief Administrator for the

Shrine, speaks about African Culture in his travels to the continent.

> I went to West Africa, Ghana, Togo and Benin. I did not go for the church
> mission on this trip. However, in Benin, we do have a church and sister village
> we support and also in Ghana. I was just visiting. It was quite an enlightened
> visit. Throughout all three countries in fact, I did not want to come back. It
> was rewarding to go visit our people and see our way of life is still being
> maintained, and I felt at home being welcomed by everyone. The social fabric
> is quite different than the west. I went to a botanical garden, which is devoted
> to medicine trees, plants and other natural things. It was very uplifting that our

---

[19] Ibid.

[20] Ifetayo Jaha Tumpe, Interviewed by Leon W. Davis tape recording, 666 Peeples Street, Atlanta, GA, 5 August 2009.

[21] Hodari Omari, Interviewed by Leon W. Davis tape recording, 667 Peeples Street, Atlanta, GA, 5 September 2009.

people are using natural medicine. The village people are still using natural medicine.[22]

On Ujimaa and cooperative economics, Brother Hodari states: "Beulah Land Farm is a multifaceted farm. It is ideally our concept of a farm. We started it in 1999; there was nothing there. We developed the infrastructure and we built the houses and bridges, roads, utilities, and brought in the office equipment. We also constructed a church there."[23] He explains the shrine and cooperative economic practice in the Shrine. "Collective economics is the basis of what we put together with Beulah Land. The concept of not going into debt to purchase the things we need. We work hard to save and put together the cash and this is why we own it because everything is paid for. We saved money for the concept of the farm. The beginning was in 1981-1982 and in 1999, we wrote a check for over 5 million dollars."[24]

Minister Ishara of the Shrine of the Black Madonna, explains African culture, and collective economics. "Beulah Land embodies the seven principles of Kwanzaa and the Nguzo Saba. It was poor people that purchased Beulah Land. When you put those things together you can accomplish what you thought you could not do alone."[25]

---

[22] Ibid.

[23] Ibid.

[24] Ibid.

[25] Minister Ishara Wright, Interviewed by Leon W. Davis tape recording, The Shrine of the Black Madonna, Atlanta, GA, 8 August 2009.

Bishop M. Fann of the Shrine of the Black Madonna explains the principles of cooperative economics Ujamaa and Ujima collective work and responsibility as practice by the Shrine.

> Collective economics is self explained. Everybody takes some responsibility for the economic welfare of the group. This means it does not matter who has the most or who has the least. The concept of collective economics means, I will participate in this economy and it benefits me whether I am rich or poor; it will benefit the entire community; Capitalism magnifies what happened in New Orleans to our people. I say that capitalism is the exploitation of man by man.[26]

Bishop Fann explains the principle of Nguzo Saba in church philosophy:

> The principles affect us throughout the years. We celebrate Kwanzaa in the church where the principles are basically taught. Each principle has a specific meaning, collective economics is one principle; unity is one of those principles. Our message is one in the Shrine where we have to understand that there is a collective responsibility to change the conditions of Black people. A lot of us are well off, a lot of us have access to that wealth. I am not playing the victim, I do not think that there is not one who has a foot on our neck saying, we can't. What I do believe is that we have been victimized psychologically so that we look to others to do for us.[27]

Black Liberation Theology

Mwalimu Diallo and the Theology of the Shrine of the Black Madonna state:

> The theology is that of Jesus being black. In his book, *the Black Messiah*, Reverend Cleage talk about the fact that Jesus was a Black Messiah and even more important is that he was a revolutionary. The fact of being black does not mean a whole lot in terms of the man. However, Jesus was trying to change the condition of the Nation of Israel. Jesus was trying to build a earthly kingdom not a heavenly kingdom.[28]

---

[26] Bishop Millton Fann, Interviewed by Leon W. Davis tape recording, The Shrine of the Black Madonna, Atlanta, GA, 8 August 2009.

[27] Ibid.

[28] Mwalimu Diallo Brown, Interviewed by Leon W. Davis tape recording, The Shrine of the Black Madonna, Atlanta, GA, 5 August 2009.

Mwalimu Diallo's response to the question of "How is God described in the Shrine's theology?" was:

> We believe that God is cosmic energy creating intelligence, which mean that everything stems from God. God is everywhere and in everything, and we believe that God is in us. The power of God is always available to us and we have to open up to it and that power which is everywhere and already here. It is in us and all around us, we have to open up to touch it.[29]

The Shrine's theological belief about African culture is expressed by Mwalimu Diallo in the quote:

> The principles of the Nguzo Saba are practices within the framework of the church. Also, the same principles were taught by Jesus the Black Messiah. Jesus taught that people need to come together. Jesus taught that the basic premise was of us being the chosen people, and we were not slaves. However, we had to gather and be self-reliant, the principles of purpose and faith that was taught by Jesus to Israel. Jesus taught that with faith, we can do all things. One of the biggest challenges that we have as a people is to believe in ourselves. If we believe in God and his power in us we can do anything.[30]
>
> I grew up in the Shrine. I was taught that the Black Nation of Israel was black, the messiah was black, Mary and the disciples were black. Also the kings in the bible were black. They were striving to liberate themselves from oppression. That theology has taught me to work in the same way. We are black people living in a system that is controlled by whites.[31]

Sister Jaribu explains the theology of liberation theology in the following statement. "The oppression of Israel is backed by facts in the Bible that the Nation of Israel was fighting against white oppression. We today, the Black Nation are fighting against that oppression."[32]   How does Jesus serve as an example for Christians today?

[29] Ibid.

[30] Ibid.

[31] Ibid.

[32] Ibid.

How does black theology of the Shrine change people to become liberators of themselves? Sister Jaribu explains the struggle in the following terms. "My understanding that the Black Messiah, Jesus is an example of what black men and women can do. The Black Messiah was born of a woman, he discovered his inner divinity; the gifts which God put in him at his birth and he went in the world and acted on those gifts."[33]

The Shrine teaches that Jesus was brought up in Egypt and was educated in their educational concept, "Man Know Thyself." Through the study of Ancient Kemet on spirituality; spirituality is reflected in the Shrine teaching on the persons, Sister Jaribu explains here, "That members must rid themselves of individualism and that part of you which is selfish and wants to look out for only yourself. You must remove individualism in order to do what is best for the group or race and dwell on the greater good. This is what Jesus stood for the greater good."[34]

Cardinal Jabari, the Shrine Administrator for the Black Madonna in Atlanta, Georgia, explains his conception of God in the Shrine theology. "When I came into the church in 1981, I did not have a clear conception of God and how God worked in the world. I began to read BCN (*Black Christian Nationalism* as well as the *Black Messiah*) both written by Rev. Albert Cleage. I have accepted this as the basis of God and how he works in the work. God is the creative source of energy and intelligence. That means

---

[33] Ifetayo Jaribu Tumpe, Interviewed by Leon W. Davis tape recording, The Shrine of the Black Madonna, Atlanta, GA 5,August 2009.

[34] Ibid.

that God permeates everything that is energy or energy force. He says, "I believe that everybody and everything vibrates on some type of energy field. That energy field is an intelligent energy field. This is what I have come to believe and accept as a basic foundation for how things work in the world."[35]

Cardinal Jabari states that the Bible is about black people. "I believe that historically it has been proven and documented that the Bible is basically about black people. The fact of it is that they are trying to become a people under the power and auspices of God. Trying to maintain the basic covenant which is I will be your God, if you will be my people. That is the basic covenant relationship."[36] Cardinal Jabari explains the historical connections of the Bible with the beginning of civilization, religion, or spirituality.

> Here today magazines such as Time magazine, etc, come out periodically showing that the Garden of Eden was in Africa. It has been documented that the oldest civilizations are in Africa. Showing it genetically showing it skeleton size, also using carbon dating of artifacts, all of these things shows that civilization was in Africa first. Before there was a political system, as we know it today, there was a theo-centric system, meaning that society was run by being what was good for God. The world's oldest civilization came out of Egypt, South Africa, Central Africa, and Ethiopia, all of this has been documented.[37]

Mwalimu Olatunji Cotton, a history instructor for the Shrine of the Black Madonna, states:

> First of all as a historian, I have to say that any research reveals that theology itself is the first spiritual teaching that comes out of Africa. It lays the

---

[35] Jabari Aritunda, Interviewed by Leon W. Davis tape recording, The Shrine of the Black Madonna, Atlanta, GA 5 August 2009.

[36] Ibid.

[37] Ibid.

foundation of what later become Christianity, Judaism and Islam. Our philosophy and theology takes us back to those early foundations. When we first as a people began to formulate ideas and a concept about God, African people were first to establish the relationship between man and God from a spiritual frame of reference.[38]

Mwalimu Olatunja also gives the historical perspective of the Shrine theology flowing

from the ancient Kemetian writings:

Yes, we can directly connect the spiritual concepts of spirituality itself to the teachings of Ptah Hotep and the *Book of the Dead* or *Book of Coming Forth by Day*. All of the major tenets related to Christianity, Judaism and Islam follows these theological precepts that are connected to the early African teachings out of ancient Kemet. Also the early African teachings from ancient African societies lead to the development of the first virgin story, the first resurrection story and all of these concepts come out of the history of religion and ancient Africa. This occurred before the establishment of Christianity, Judaism or Islam. Also the life of Ausar or Osiris paralleled the life of Jesus and was written thousands of years before the birth of Jesus.[39]

Mwalmu Olatunji maintains:

The foundation of the Shrine liberation theology, all of the concepts mentioned comes out of African spirituality and form of basis of our theology which is our foundation at the Shrine. So you take the basic concepts and understanding and make them relevant to the time we live in today.[40]

On the question of "What is your understanding of Reverend Cleage's book, *The*

Black Messiah and how it relates to the Theology of the Shrine?," Olatunji explains that

"The Black Messiah has been a vehicle not only to help us understand our program and

philosophy but it also helps our people around the world to understand our historical

relationship to the Bible. The theology we use today is used by the Black church

---

[38] Mwalimu Olilunji Cotton, Interviewed by Leon W. Davis tape recording, The Shrine of the Black Madonna, Atlanta, GA, 15 March 2009.

[39] Ibid.

[40] Ibid.

traditionally to understand our historical reality."[41]   Mwalimu Olatunji relates the book

Black Messiah to black people in general, when he contends that "It is not only for us but

for other conscious brothers and sisters around the world to get an understanding of

African history, culture and tradition especially as it flows out of our spiritual reality that

we have as a people."[42]

Cardinal Mwende Brown is the CEO and Pastor of the Shrine in Atlanta. Mwende

Brown states the theology of the Shrine in the following passages.

> Our understanding of Black Theology as taught by the Shrine is to look at the
> Bible from a historical perspective as the Bible has been taught from the
> Eurocentric perspective traditionally in the Western churches. The Shrine's
> understanding of the Bible and how it relates to our lives as Black people is
> where we begin to look at the Bible from an African perspective. And the Shrine
> uses it as a liberation theology. The Bible is our rule of faith, but we do take a
> critical perspective at how the Bible and its teaching aid us as a group.[43]

Cardinal Mwende defines the new theology when he maintains, "So we bring an

African or a black interpretation to the Bible. This is how the Shrine has been

instrumental during the days of Albert Cleage, when he was really beginning to push

back from the Eurocentric interpretation and to deposit a black liberation theology."[44]

The book, the *Black Messiah*, is a collection of Reverend Cleage's sermons. In these

sermons, we begin to see Reverend Cleage's ideas as they play out in terms of how it

correlates the Shrine Theology and Reverend Cleage's understanding of the Bible.

---

[41] Ibid.

[42] Ibid.

[43] Mwende Brown, Interviewed by Leon W. Davis tape recording, The Shrine of the Black Madonna, Atlanta, GA, 12 March 2009.

[44] Ibid.

Rev. Cleage brings the position and location of Black people in conversation with the Bible and so by doing this, he does not leave the Bible in isolation, nor does he leave the black experience in isolation. He places the two in conversation with each other. The understanding that we are able to glean from the Bible and those practical things that will help us in our day to day struggle as a group of people, but being about understanding the Black Messiah and look at how the church construct it's theology.[45]

The theology of the Shrine states that God is cosmic energy. Cardinal Mwende explains this in the next statements.

So we get to look at God as a cosmic energy of intelligence. It begins to remind us that everything in the universe is energy and that we have impact on how energy is experienced and exchanged. Inside of the worship space we come to bring our individual energies to this particular worship experience. We have impact, we have come with the intent of being able to communicate with the transcendent reality we call God.[46]

"The Bible through Jesus speaks of how God is one with his being. The father and I have become one. It is just energy he has aligned; thus, he has aligned himself with the energy that permeates the universe."[47]

Ifetayo Jaha Tumpe gives her understanding of the Shrine's theology of liberation in simple terms. She explains that "We believe that Jesus was a man, a messiah, he is no different from us and therefore we can accomplish and achieve great things just like what he accomplished. We do not believe like some religions that Jesus is God and we believe that God is within and around us. Also Jesus was a Black Messiah and we are all Black Messiahs. The ones that come after us are Black Messiahs and we really believe that based on where Jesus was born, his mother was of African descent and there is where the

---

[45] Ibid.

[46] Ibid.

[47] Ibid.

name Black Madonna come from, also the whole black theology is based on that history."[48]

The Shrine's interpretation of Jesus as a revolutionary speaks to the actions of the church in politics and religion. Sister Tumpe describes Jesus in his role in liberation theology when she says "Yes, again in traditional churches, they seem to give the impression that Jesus basically dies for our sins but we see Jesus as a revolutionary. When you think of some of the Bible stories, it talks about Jesus going in to the temple overthrowing the tables and throwing them out, the Pharisees of the temple, since they should be there to worship."[49]

Tumpe is describing the only time in the life of Jesus where he is using physical violence against the people who were cooperating with the system. The role of Jesus as a revolutionary activist is captured in her story of how Jesus tried to change the condition of his people Israel that were oppressed by the Romans.

> Jesus was a revolutionary, he wanted to change things, and he was not just a meek little person, who sat around. He shook up the community, this basically what we should be doing. Our goal should be to shake up the community to make things right to accomplish and do for our people as opposed to sitting around waiting for someone to come and do it for us. So that is how we see Jesus, the Black Messiah, and certainly the church has been more revolutionary in the past. There is still the need for us to be revolutionary and try to liberate our people. Liberation is very important. A people cannot be strong unless they are liberated.[50]

---

[48] Ifetayo Jabiru Tumpe, Interviewed by Leon W. Davis, tape recording, 666 Peeples Street, Atlanta, GA 5 August 2009.

[49] Ibid.

[50] Ibid.

In response to the question of "What is your knowledge of the Black theology as taught by the Shrine?, Cardinal Hodari stated, "The first thing is to acknowledge the historical blackness of Jesus. This is where we get the Black Madonna of the Shrine, which is a historical fact. The Shrine teaches Black liberation theology, our God want us to struggle for freedom. It is a sin to be enslaved and not struggle against your slave master."[51] The type of Christianity taught by the Shrine is reflected in Cardinal Hodari statement of the Shrine's concept of what is the real Christianity and those ideals that are a distortion.

> The Shrine's concept of Christianity is a black religion that was established with the same Bible most people use also. It was established in Jesus disciples at the Pentecost. The Shrine differs from most other religious practices. We believe that Jesus and all his disciples were black people, and placed over the original black Nation of Israel. There is a history to base that on.[52]

Cardinal Hodari gives an example of the teaching that separates progressive Christianity from the one taught by western churches. "Peter actually did accomplish things beyond what Jesus did, at the Pentecost. He became so powerful that his shadow when it came upon you, would heal you."[53]

Minister Ishara Metra Wright talks about the theology of the Shrine in the following passages.

> We certainly call ourselves Christians, we are Pan African Orthodox Christians. This is what I have learned in the church, Christianity is an African religion, Jesus is the Black Messiah. His mission was to uplift and to empower the Black

---

[51] Ibid.

[52] Ibid.

[53] Ibid.

Israel Nation. Our theology is to extract what Jesus was trying to do in his mission and to apply that to what we are trying to do for black people as well.[54]

The Reverend Milton C. Fann is poetic in his description of the theology of the Shrine. He gives a simple interpretation of the theology of the Shrine.

> Black theology simply means we try and look at our religion through the context of our black experience. Black theology is not anything new, it was initiated by Rev. Cleage. It is our understanding of Black theology that God work within the context of the Black man and coming from a period of slavery, where we were given a certain conceptualization and belief by the enemy system. A white system that was controlled by white people and their interpretation of our relationship with God was servitude and a humbleness toward them. We were told to obey our master rather than standing up for ourselves; independent of our need for others as well as creating a certain separation and dependency on others rather than ourselves.[55]

Black Nationalism

The Shrine of the Black Madonna defines its Black Nationalism as the call for black people to commit themselves to the possibility of building a black communal society here on earth. This is achieved by accepting the Black Christian Nationalism (BCN) training and discipline necessary to free the mind from individualism and materialism. The members are laboring to restructure the black church to provide a power base for the systematic building of the black nation.[56]

---

[54] Ishara Metra Wright, Interviewed by Leon W. Davis tape recording, The Shrine of the Black Madonna, Atlanta, GA, 12 August 2009.

[55] Rev. Milton C. Fann, Interviewed by Leon W. Davis tape recording, The Shrine of the Black Madonna, Atlanta, GA, 28 July 2009.

[56] Albert Cleage, Black Christian Nationalism, 204.

The church uses the term Pan-Africanism as the ultimate realization of the movement. It is Pan-Africanist and its basic loyalty is to the worldwide unity of black people and to the liberation of the motherland, Africa.[57] The goal of Black Nationalism as stated in the words of Mwalimu Diallo is: "The Book BCN set a direction for the black church. The Black Nationalism of BCN or Black Christian Nationalism's goal is to build a black nation. The goal of the black church should be to build the nation, and Black Nationalism is to bring in to being and build the nation through the power of God.[58] Jaribu Chitunda states the Shrine is dedicated to black nationalism in the following phrase, "So a lot of the philosophy in the revealed religions gets their roots and origins in Africa. However, to be a Black Christian Nationalist is to believe in nationhood and that black people can be one nation and be unified to do things for the black race."[59]

The question of what is the difference between black nationalism and black Christian nationalism is answered by Cardinal Jabari in his statement. "You have Black Nationalism where black people want black power and to be able to control their own institutions and do for self. Black Christian Nationalism is an added element where we want to have our own institutions and they come out of our expression of what we want

---

[57] Ibid.

[58] Mwalimu Diallo, Interview by Leon W. Davis tape recording, The Shrine of the Black Madonna, Atlanta, GA, 5 August 2009.

[59] Jaribu Chitunda, Interviewed by Leon W. Davis tape recording, The Shrine of the Black Madonna, Atlanta, GA, 8 August 2009.

to be. The Christian element allows the people to be human in their response to each other."[60]

Cardinal Mwende Brown in an effort to give the direction of Black Christian Nationalism as it relates to the Black churches asserts the following:

> So that inside of the black church Christian nationalist says that the church has to be a spin off institution that creates the holistic environment for black people to function. It is not just for your soul only but also to finance and to create a value system and those other institutions that are necessary for your survival has to be a spin off from the church. The black church is challenged to become a dominant part of the mechanism for nation building and not just a Sunday institution. The Beulah Land project is an attempt of the church to supply a basic need of the people. Cardinal Mwende states what the black Christian nationalist believe to be the foundation for Nation maintenance in their teachings.

Cardinal Brown also suggests that "If you read the book Black Christian Nationalism it talks about a nation within a nation. We have to build power for ourselves; we have to build a nation within a nation, even though we are inside the United States."[61]

The idea that black people represented a nation within a nation is simply the description offered by other nationalist thinkers such as Malcolm X and Kwame Toure who said that black people in America were the victims of domestic colonialism. The black nation of the Republic of New Africa (RNA) has the prototype structure of a nation in transition from a colony to a republic. The RNA was established to function as the government of the black nation within the United States. Cardinal Hodari states that religion was used to enslave black people in the world. The Black Christian nationalists

---

[60] Cardinal Jabari, Interviewed by Leon W Davis tape recording, The Shrine of the Black Madonna, Atlanta, GA, 8 August 2009.

[61] Cardinal Mwende Brown, Interviewed by Leon W. Davis tape recording, The Shrine of the Black Madonna, Atlanta, GA , 12 March 2009.

are true nationalists wanting to build a black nation.[62] He continues to describe the tendency of the enemy to try and divide the black people in the United States into separatists and integrationists. However, Cardinal Hodari states that nationalism has become a key verbiage of separation. It was a term used during the 1960s to try to solidify the collective interest of black people.[63]

Communalism

The Shrine of the Black Madonna has adopted the African economic system of communalism; whereas, the African attitude toward social relations is practiced in some African societies today. In a speech in New York, to the African community, Kwame Ture states that there are only two systems of economics, capitalism, and socialism. Under capitalism, only a few people own the means of production or wealth. In the economy under socialism, everyone owns the means of production or the wealth of the nation. The idea of communalism is the father of socialism. It basically rests in Africa for a long period of time. The traditional African society was communal.

The economic system used by the Shrine is modeled on the African communal system. One African communal system is practiced by the LUO Tribe of Kenya. Their idea of communalism is that it is not based on sharing property or wealth. Their idea of communalism is of a cooperative nature. The idea of communalism is expressed in the reality of everyone having what they need to live. There is no private ownership of

---

[62] Cardinal Hodari, Interviewed by Leon W. Davis, tape recording, The Shrine of the Black Madonna, Atlanta, GA, 12, September 2009.

[63] Ibid.

wealth that exploits those who are not as fortunate as some. The idea that whatever one needs is satisfied by the community through cooperative economics as expressed in the Kwanzaa term Ujamaa.

Julius K. Nyere, in his essay "Ujamaa–The Basis of African Socialism," states clearly, this is the same position of the Shrine on communalism, or socialism; "Socialism, like democracy is an attitude of mind. In a socialist society it is the socialist attitude of mind and not the rigid adherence to a standard political pattern, which is needed to ensure that people care for each other's welfare."[64] The Shrine of the Black Madonna corrected the individualism of the member so they could have a communalistic state of mind.

Mwalimu Diallo expressed the idea of the extended family and the idea of collective communal living and how it will affect the nation. He says that "The communal living is outside the church, where as we can pool lour resources, we also have expenses. In terms of communalism, you get an opportunity to share and grow and to develop along with your brothers and sisters. You will be with people of like mind and you can work together and accomplish a lot more."[65]

The attitude of mind of socialism as described by Julius Nyere is also reflected in Mwalimu Diallo's comments on Beulah Land. "In terms of collective economics Beulah Land could not have come into being without the collective efforts of everyone in the church. Once the institution is fully developed, the benefits in terms of the things that are

---

[64] Julius Nyere, Ujama, The Basis of African Socialism, Ed. Fred Lee Hood and Johnathan Scott Lee, I am because We are (Amherst, University of Massachusetts Press 1995), 65

[65] Ibid.

produced on Beulah Land will benefit the Black Nation as a whole. We really need to develop Beulah Land in order to maintain and sustain the Black Nation."[66]

Mwalimu Diallo gives a clear picture of why blacks are suffering. He states: "The reason we suffer, today is because we do not pool our resources we do not support our own stores, and we provide jobs and opportunities for other people rather than for ourselves."[67] The attitude of the Shrine that reflects African socialism is reflected in the ideas of Mwalimu Diallo description of the attitude of members of the Shrine. "In our communalism, we reject a lot of materialism because it is less expensive to live. We submerge ourselves with this atmosphere and there is no individualism. Individualism is eliminated and it eliminates the need to escape an illusion because there are no drugs."[68]

The attitude of the Shrine members is that things shall be in harmony and create prosperity for the black nation in America. The attitude is a necessity for them to be free and independent people in the land of plenty. The task is executed to avoid the advantages and disadvantages of the capitalist system; whereas, black people will not be affected too harshly when the system takes a down turn.

Cardinal Jabari reflects on Beulah Land and communalism in his own words as follows:

> Beulah Land is a very positive expression of what people can do when they respond as a group, and what they believe in and are able to carry out over years. This was not a vision that took place in two or three years, we were on this for 10

---

[66] Mwalimu Diallo interviewed by Leon W. Davis tape recording, The Shrine of the Black Madonna, Atlanta, GA, 9 August 2009.

[67] Ibid.

[68] Ibid.

years or more. This was a vision of the founder of the church. The concept of give as you have and receive as needed is the concept that is a part of the communal lifestyle.[69]

The practice of communalism is very important to the Shrine because it begins to instill in each member an Afrocentric concept of Africanity. Mwalimu Olatuniji describes how communalism brings members back to themselves and destroys the ideas of western individualism. Olatunji states:

> The communalism experience starts when you first join the church. You are assigned to a group. You have a group of individuals who have been trained by western individualism to look out for themselves and only to sometimes look out their immediate families. When we come to the church we are assigned to groups and we have to relearn how to love one another. We learn how to work collectively with one another and how to resolve disputes we might have in a positive and constructive way.[70]

The main way the Shrine goes about changing their members to accept a new attitude is described by Mwalimu Olatunji in these words. "It is the training process of relearning, how to belong to one another. Other communal practices help to reinforce this—meals, rituals, outings, fellowship, and living together where we have residential housing. We also cook for one another, serve each other, take care of our children together and teach and heal each other. This kind of communal reality helps strengthen us as a people and is an integral part of being an African."[71]

---

[69] Cardinal Jabari, Interviewed by Leon W.Davis tape recording, The Shrine of the Black Madonna, Atlanta, GA,3 March 2009.

[70] Cardinal Jabari, Interviewed by Leon W. Davis tape recording, The Shrine of the Black Madonna, Atlanta, GA, 3March 2009.

[71] Mwalimu Olatunji, Interviewed by Leon W..Davis, tape recording, The Shrine of the Black Madonna, Atlanta, GA, 15 March 2009.

The effect of communalism on the members is expressed by the relationships between members. The communal living is very effective in bringing people together for a common solution to the problem of people trying to build a nation within a nation. Cardinal Mwende Brown expresses:

> We have people who share common experience and common values. That experience is like nothing I have experienced when I was growing up as a kid. Everyone in the community knew each other. Inside this living environment the values you embrace in terms of communal values is a realized experience you see and you participate in it. Therefore, it does not seem that the values are strong because you are in an environment where that particular value system is actively embraced.[72]

The communal living experience is the key to the members of the Shrine becoming an extended family. The communal values of the Shrine are expressed by Cardinal Brown in his statement: "Collective economics is self explained, everybody takes some responsibility for the economic welfare of the group. This means it does not matter who has the most or who has the least. The concept of collective economics means I will participate in this economy and it will benefit me if I am rich or poor."[73] The Shrine members take on the problems as their own because they have a philosophy of "I am, because we are."

Transformation

The idea of transformation as expressed by Bishop Fann is that transformation and salvation are the same. The three processes by which individuals are able to

---

[72] Cardinal Mwende Brown, Interviewed by Leon W. Davis tape recording. The Shrine of the Black Madonna, Atlanta, GA, 12 March 2009.

[73] Ibid.

submerge their individualism and become a part of a group experience are stated by Reverend Cleage in the book *Black Christian Nationalism* on page 73. They are: (1) the process by which the individual is transformed through a national group experience in which he must face reality as mirrored in group confrontation, criticism and love; (2) The process by which the individual is transformed through the emotional experience of a rhythmic African religious ceremony deliberately designed to break down the walls of individualism; and (3) The sudden Pentecostal experience which occurs unexpectedly when the walls of individualism have been eroded quietly through sustained, deeply emotional group experience over an extended period of time.[74]

What is it that the Shrine has to transform in the black community? Is it the slave culture that exists in the black community, or is it the oppressive white culture that deforms the black man's culture in the United States? One could suggest that African-American life is deformed by the white oppression of black people.

The ideal of black liberation is not new. The fight to overcome slavery in the United States began the moment nineteen Africans left the boat in Jamestown in 1619. Transformation, as seen by the members and leaders of the Shrine, should be observed in the following examination of their interviews. The answers to the questions on the KUA System which was explained in Chapter One and in the interview questions are now examined.

---

[74] Bishop Milton Fann, Interviewed by Leon W. Davis tape recording, The Shrine of the Black Madonna, Atlanta, GA, 28 July 2009.

Mwalimu Diallo answers the following questions. What were your interpretations of the KUA groups? How did the KUA groups move people from individualism to collective identity or communalism? He states:

> The KUA devotional gives an individual a chance to do self reflection. In order to change ourselves and change the world in which we live, we have to look at ourselves and the change has to begin within. We also understand that salvation is a group process and change can only come through groups, that is why you have groups such as Al –Anon, Macabees, etc, where it takes a group of people to come and institute change. KUA helps an individual get in touch with his or her inner self so he or she can move beyond his present state.

Mwalmu Diallo described the process Rev. Cleage identified in his three processes of overcoming individualism.[75]

Sister Jaribu, a member of the church choir, describes transformation in terms of how her position in the Shrine helps in her understanding of the vision of the Shrine. She says that "As far as the vision of transformation, our vision is transforming the minds of black people through these different avenues. We are able to facilitate that process whether assisting in group meeting or interacting with one another on a daily basis. It teaches us how to work together and how to give constructive criticism when necessary. It is to correct one another to hold people to the standard of being a Black Christian Nationalist or to the standard of being a Christian."[76]

Sister Jaribu gives an interesting answer to the questions on the KUA groups. She states, "KUA is the art of becoming. It includes different aspects of artificial barriers

---

[75] Ibid.

[76] Ifetayo Jaribu Tumpe, Interviewed by Leon W. Davis tape recording, The Shrine of the Black Madonna, Atlanta, GA, 9 August 2009.

which are breaking down walls of separation. We have small devotionals; we participate in vocations, mediation, encounter discourse about God, singing and all those things that will allow those walls of separation to erode. And this allows us to feel a collective identity as one and those KUA devotional small groups impact me in that I always felt empowered and connected to the people in those groups. We build relationships that are long lasting."[77]

Mwalimu Olatunji gives an example of what people in the Shrine call slave community. He states:

> The slave culture we understand it. However we are the counter culture. The slave culture is the culture where you basically are out for yourself. You are not thinking about the greater good or the whole of the group, you are being materialistic and what you can get for yourself. The slave culture is different. It is not looking out for your brother just looking out for yourself. It is the type of slave culture that we are prohibited from spending a lot of time in. It is the opposite of looking out for one another. In the slave culture, people can write you off. In the counter culture, we do not write you off, we are all we have. It goes back to I Am because We are.[78]

Cardinal Jabari statement of the KUA group's process is as follows:

> The KUA groups develop into what is known as a devotional. It is a seven step process that groups will go through. On the one hand, we will evoke the presence of God; it will give us an understanding of the nature of God. There will be awareness, exercises that would give you a greater understanding of your better need for each other. So that on the one hand clarity was brought in the understanding of the nature of God. It teaches you the interdependence of everything in the world.[79]

---

[77] Ibid.

[78] Mwalimu Olatunji Cotton, Interviewed by Leon W. Davis tape recording, The Shrine of the Black Madonna, Atlanta, GA, 15 March 2009.

[79] Jabari Henry, Interviewed by Leon W. Davis tape recording, The Shrine of the Black Madonna, Atlanta, GA, 3 March 2009.

Cardinal Mwende Brown is prophetic in his understanding of the transformation

process as practiced by the small groups within the Shrine. He states:

> The KUA system is a transformational system. It is a process we go through,
> part of the process is a small group experience. Our founder realized that in our
> history because we are African people, we function better in groups. The groups
> serve as an incubator for the socialization process as well. The KUA small
> groups experience allows us to come into a setting where other people can mirror
> back to us behaviors that we can see ourselves and its break down the walls of
> isolation or individualism that we picked up from western culture. Cardinal
> Mwende also gives the strength of small group interactions that occur in the
> KUA groups. He states, The small groups are very important because the small
> groups are trying to instill the values of African communalism. I am because we
> are. The transformation process is accelerated because you have a group of
> people who are working on change, rather than one individual trying to do it
> alone.[80]

The transformation process can be described as the life of a worm that becomes a

butterfly through transformation. The butterfly changes its conditions and rises as a free

entity that is no longer defenseless. The worm is transformed by weaving a cocoon that

is a shell. Then, it emerges after sometime as a butterfly that has overcome his handicap

of little mobility on the ground into a mobile butterfly that soars in the sky to live the life

of freedom. The neophyte of the KUA groups is transformed into the freedom fighter

that transcends the limits of individualism to be part of the new nation that is free and self

determining.

Cardinal Mwende describes the process of transforming as the Bible described the

experience of the Pentecost of the Christian church, and the first disciples of Jesus.

When the rush of the mighty wind filled the upper room and the tongues of fire sat upon

---

[80] Cardinal Mwende Brown, Interviewed by Leon W. Davis tape recording, The Shrine of the
Black Madonna, Atlanta, GA 12 March 2009.

the head of the people at Pentecost and transformed them into miracle workers by

enabling them to do things that even Jesus did not do. Peter was one of such people.

> We have what you call the Pentecostal experience; it is not just a one time thing where the fire is set upon each head, but it is an ongoing Pentecostal experience. Inside the group it is this transforming process that takes place over time. Inside this group experience it is this idea that I can have a continuous Pentecostal experience. I feel the rush of the mighty wind in terms of fire resting on every head. Because it is the coming together of the rhythmic process that we begin to erode the walls of individualism that separate us one from another and also from God.[81]

Sister Ifetoya Jaribu Tumpe gives examples of how the group experience changed

her forever in a positive and meaningful way. She maintains that "The KUA group is a

powerful thing; it is about mind, body, and spirit; it introduces you to meditation. If you

are participating in a KUA group you get to learn about and understand the people, and it

is not on the surface level. You really get to know and bond with these people."[82] Sister

Ifetoya also describes how the group experience changed her relationship with family and

friends. "It has changed me in a positive way. I have a different attitude toward life. A

lot of black churches focus on the hereafter, my focus is right here on earth. I focus on

what happened while I am alive and how I can make the world a better place while I am

alive."[83]

Interview Questions

1. What is your position in the Shrine and how has it aided your understanding of the vision of the Shrine?

---

[81] Ibid.

[82] Ifetoyo Jaribu Tumpe , Interviewed by Leon W. Davis tape recording, The Shrine of the Black Madonna, Atlanta, GA, 5 August 2009.

[83] Ibid.

2. What is your knowledge of Black theology as taught by the Shrine?

3. What is your understanding of Rev. Cleage's book, *Black Messiah*, and how it relates to the Theology of the Shrine?

4. What is your understanding of Rev. Cleage's book, *BCN-Black Christian Nationalism*, and how it relates to black nationalism?

5. How has your participation in the Church Synods helped your vision of the future of the Shrine?

6. What were your interpretations of the KUA groups and how they moved people from individualism to collective identity? Ex: "I am because we are, we are because I am?"

7. How does the collective communal living experience in the Shrine affect you?

8. Describe Beulah Land Farms? How has Beulah land Farms influences your views of collective economics and its benefits? What is your perception of collective economics?

9. How has the worship service influenced you in helping you to obtain a collective spiritual experience with the Supreme Being as a cosmic energy field? Provide a description of communal life. In what ways has communal living impacted your views of black needs and black levels of black consciousness?

10. How have the Nguzo Saba Principles created by Maulana Karenga been experienced by you and its effect on the programs of the Shrine?

11. In what ways do the teachings of the Shrine impact your life outside of the Shrine?

Quantitative Findings

The qualitative findings as presented in the preceding section of this chapter are directly related to the quantitative findings. They are: (1) African Culture; (2) Black Liberation Theology; (3) Black Nationalism; (4) Transformation; and (5) Communalism.

The basis of the quantitative findings section is based upon the four factors in Baldwin's Afrocentric personality test: (1) collection African identity and Self-fortification (2) resistance against anti-African forces, (3) value for African centered institutions and cultural expression, and (4) value for African culture.

The first Baldwin factor is African Identity and Self-Fortification. The response of the interviews to the questions begins with the researcher's analysis of the category of African Culture. The researcher used the Nguzo Saba principles to measure and analyze the interview responses for African Culture. The seven principles of the Nguzo Saba are (1) Umoja – Unite; (2) Kujichagulia – Self Determination; (3) Ujimaa – Collective Work and Responsibility; (4) Ujamaa – Cooperative Economics; (5) Nia – Purpose; (6) Kuumba – Creativity; and (7) Imani – Faith. Secondly, for another Baldwin factor of African resistance to anti-African forces, the researcher correlated the interview response to the question pertaining to Black Liberation Theology. Thirdly, the Baldwin principle of Value for Afrocentric institutions and cultural expression could be represented by the category for the survey analysis of Black Nationalism as expressed by the Shrine Land Holdings for Beulah Land. Baldwin's fourth factor of values for African culture were correlated to the category of communalism as expressed in the survey by the respondent on the practice of communal living and their practice of being transformed from individual to collective identification in the KUA group concept of "I Am Because We Are."

African Self-Consciousness Scale (ASCS) Instructions

The ASC Scale is a 42-item questionnaire (in its original form) developed by Kambon and Associates. In 1996, the scale is conceptually organized into four competency dimensions of African self-consciousness and six manifest dimensions of education, family, religion, cultural activities, interpersonal relations and political orientation. The four ASC competencies are: (1) awareness/recognition of one's African identity and heritage; (2) general ideological and activity priorities placed on black survival, liberation and proactive/affirmative development; (3) specific activity priorities placed on self-knowledge, Afrocentric values, customs and institutions; and (4) a posture of resolute resistance/ defense against anti-black forces and threats to black survival in general. These four competencies correspond to the four ASCS subfactors/ subscales of F1 - Collective African Identity, F2 - Resistance/Defense against anti-African Forces, F3 - Value for Afrocentric institutions and Cultural Expressions, and F4 - Value for African Culture. Around 90 percent of the items were loaded on these four factors, accounting for nearly 76 percent of the variability. Cronbach Alpha coefficients for the ASCS range from .79 to .82, while test-retest reliability coefficients covering intervals from six weeks up to nine months occur well within the high 80s to low 90s range.

The African Self-Consciousness Scale Scoring Key

The ASC Scale is structured such that every other item is weighted or keyed in the opposite direction for ASC, alternating from Negative to Positive keys. Thus, for Positive keyed items, high scores (above 4) are indicative of strong/high ASC, and for Negative keyed items, low scores (4 and below) are indicative of strong/high ASC. Therefore, Negative (Odd numbered) item scores must be transposed to their ASC weights or values. For example, a Negative weighted score of 1 is converted/transposed to 8, a 2 to 7, 3 to 6, etc. (i.e., a Negative weighted

item $1 = 8$, $2 = 7$, $3 = 6$, $4 = 5$, $5 = 4$, $6 = 3$, $7 = 2$, $8 = 1$).

Factor I. Collective African Identity and Self-Fortification: Items 1, 2, 4, 6, 10, 12, 14, 16, 18, 23, 26, 30, 36, 40, 42 (15 items)

Factor II. Resistance Against Anti-African Forces: Items 3, 8, 9, 13, 15, 17, 31, 32, 33, 37, 41 (11 items)

Factor III. Value for African-Centered Institutions and Cultural Expressions: Items 20, 22, 24, 25, 27, 29, 34, 39 (8 items)

Factor IV. Value for African Culture: Items 5, 7, 19, 21, 28 (5 items)

Total ASCS Scoring Range = 42 - 336 Points
Mid-Point/Mean Score = 168 Points
High ASCS Score Range = 252 -336 Points
Middle ASCS Score Range = 127 -251 Points
Low ASCS Score Range = 42-126 Points

F1 Scoring Range = 15 - 120 Points
High Range = 75.5 - 120
Low Range = 15 - 75

F2 Scoring Range = 11 - 88 Points
High Range = 55.5 - 88
Low Range = 11 - 55

F3 Scoring Range = 8 - 64 Points
High Range = 40.5 - 64
Low Range = 8 – 40
F4 Scoring Range = 5 - 40 Points
High Range = 20.5 - 40
Low Range = 5 – 20

The African Self-Consciousness Scale: Four Factors

    Factor 1: Collective African Identity and Self-Fortification—A psychological disposition reflecting a sense of collective African identity and a tendency to engage in activities that affirm one's African identity, (e.g., pro-black/black empowering actions like promoting African history and cultural activities; black organized/collective activities, black economic and political activities/Nguzo Saba, etc.)

    Factor 2: Resistance Against Anti-African Forces—A psychological disposition reflecting a tendency to resist, by any means necessary, any and all information which may be perceived (experienced/interpreted) as anti-African/anti-black, or as a threat to African or black survival in any way, shape or form, (e.g., rejects white supremacy and actively combats it in all areas of experience.)

    Factor 3: Value for African-Centered Institutions and Cultural Expressions—A psychological disposition reflecting a belief in the importance of Afrocentric/pro-black-oriented/empowering organizations-institutions and practices that are under African/black control based on African cultural definitions, (e.g., practicing African cultural rituals, celebrations, and commemorations)

    Factor 4: Value for African Culture—A psychological disposition reflecting a firm belief in the value/importance of traditional African cultural forms (practices, products-artifacts, etc.) for Africans (in America).

    Scores of 40 respondents on the four factors tested on the ASCS test are presented in Table 1. The results of 36 respondents were in the high range of Factor I and four respondents were in the low range. The mean score is 93.6 (high range).

Table 1. Responses to Four Factors of the ASC Scale survey

Respondent	Factor I High (75.5 – 120) Low (15 – 75)	Factor II High (55.5 – 88) Low (11- 55)	Factor III High (40.5 – 64) Low (8 – 40)	Factor IV High (20.5 – 40) Low (5 – 20)
1	106	64	51	35
2	112	72	61	40
3	108	70	52	36
4	120	78	61	40
5	88	60	44	34
6	105	79	56	32
7	99	84	46	25
8	103	59	46	31
9	112	81	59	38
10	115	82	58	38
11	105	75	43	35
12	73	62	36	26
13	98H.HH	66	49	26
14	101	35	40	16
15	57	74	43	30
16	93	77	53	36
17	96	54	46	35
18	68	52	40	36
19	109	77	56	28
20	102	80	57	30
21	73	52	40	34
22	81	68	47	28
23	96	75	44	30
24	95	68	46	27
25	95	68	58	36
26	112	85	63	34
27	100	56	42	33
28	94	79	39	34
29	90	65	43	32
30	87	78	45	32
31	83	60	42	34
32	109	80	46	35
33	69	82	44	30
34	107	88	63	37
35	108	77	54	39
36	79	67	49	28
37	94	74	56	30
38	80	41	34	20
39	110	75	58	35
40	105	72	53	26

For Factor II, 35 respondents tested in the high range for this factor and five

respondents tested in the low range. The mean score = 65.9 (high range). For Factor III,

there were 37 respondents that tested in the high range and the mean score = 49.1 (high

range). For Factor IV, there were 38 respondents who tested in the high range and two

respondents tested in the low range. The mean score = 32 (high range).

Mean Scores of Respondents by Factor

Factor I: African ID and Self Fortification—Mean Score = 94.6
Factor II: Resistance to Anti-African Forces—Mean Score = 65.9
Factor III: Value for African Centered Institutions and Cultural Expression—
                 Mean Score = 49.1
Factor IV: Value for African Culture—Mean Score = 32

Total ASCS Score for all 40 respondents overall mean = 253.9

The total raw scores of African Consciousness on the ASCS were: Low = 41-

126; Middle = 127-251, and High = 257-336. The total scores of ASCS for 40

respondents scoring for overall African Self Consciousness Scale: 26 scores were

recorded in the high range of African Consciousness; 14 respondents had scores in the

middles range for total score of African Self-Consciousness and the ASCS. None of

them were in the low range. The mean score for overall ASCS scores: 253.9 (high

range) (see Table 2).

Table 2. Total Raw Score: African Self-Consciousness

Respondent	Score
1	Total: ASCS 268 High Range
2	Total ASCS 237 High Range
3	Total ASCS 266 High Range
4	Total ASCS 252 High Range

(continued)

Table 2 (continued)

Respondent	Score
5	Total ASCS 239 Middle Range
6	Total ASCS 225 High Range
7	Total ASCS 277 High Range
8	Total ASCS 252 High Range
9	Total ASCS 252 High Range
10	Total ASCS 252 High Range
11	Total ASCS 252 Middle Range
12	Total ASCS 251 Middle Range
13	Total ASCS 256 High Range
14	Total ASCS 127 Middle Range
15	Total ASCS 127 Middle
16	Total ASCS 272 High Range
17	Total ASCS 127 Middle Range
18	Total ASCS 211 Middle Range
19	Total ASCS 252 High Range
20	Total ASCS 287 High Range
21	Total ASCS 127 Middle Range
22	Total ASCS 127 Middle Range
23	Total ASCS 262 High Range
24	Total ASCS 127 Middle Range
25	Total ASCS 252 High Range
26	Total ASCS 252 High Range
27	Total ASCS 127 Middle Range
28	Total ASCS 252 High Range
29	Total ASCS 127 Middle Range
30	Total ASCS 127 Middle Range
31	Total ASCS 127 Middle Range
32	Total ASCS 22 High Range
33	Total ASCS 232 Middle Range
34	Total ASCS 312 High Range
35	Total ASCS 292 High Range
36	Total ASCS 237 Middle Range
37	Total ASCS 270 High Range
38	Total ASCS 184 Middle Range
39	Total ASCS 287 High Range
40	Total ASCS 274 High Range

ASCS: 11, 35, 38
Low: 41-126 Middle: 127-251 High: 252-336
Total Score of ASCS for 40 respondents scoring for High Middle and Low Range

Table 3 presents the high to low range on the four factors and Table 4 shows the total ASC score for the 40 respondents.

Table 3. High to Low Range on the Four Factors

Range	Factor I	Factor II	Factor III	Factor IV
High Range	35	35	34	38
Low Range	5	5	6	2

Table 4: Total ASC Score for 40 Respondents

High	Middle	Low
24	16	0

High Range 252-336
Middle Range 127 – 251
Low Range 42 - 127

The number of High Range Scores was 26. There were 14 Middle Range scores for the total 40 respondents. The degree of high range was larger than the middle range with none of the respondents scoring in the low range area.

The findings for the survey of Baldwin's African Self-Consciousness Scale conclude that the 40 respondents score in the high range for the four factors measured by the instrument. The 40 respondents were on the upper level of the measured factors and had a high range score for overall African self-consciousness. The 40 respondents had a high degree of African-Centered Consciousness. The personality of the 40 respondents, as it is measured by the survey, shows that they are highly Afrocentric. The survey, as it is indicated in the qualitative interviews and the five categories derive from the interviews, show that 40 respondents were conscious of their African centered program of the Shrine of the Black Madonna.

The African Self-Consciousness Scale Questions Analysis

The questions on Baldwin's Afrocentric personality test have factors that measure the respondents on four different factors which are the African Identity and Self Fortification, the Anti-African Resistance, the Identification with Afrocentric Institution and Cultural Expressions, and the Value for African Culture.

The 15 questions that measure the African identity and self fortification were represented by the following question on the test or survey: Should black people have their own independent schools which consider their African heritage and values an important part of the curriculum? The highest score in the factor was 120 and the lowest was 57. The respondents tended to score high on this factor in the survey.

The second factor measured was the resistance against anti-African forces. The African Self Consciousness Scale by Baldwin that recorded the responses on this factor was represented by the following question: Are blacks who trust whites in general basically very intelligent beings? In dealing with other blacks, the researcher considers himself quite different and unique from most of them.

The respondents had a range for the highest score on these 11 questions from 88 to the lowest score of 35. The score for the 40 respondents overall on this factor was not as good as that of the previous factor. There were more low range scores for this factor than on the first factor of African Identity.

The African Self-Consciousness Scale test or survey had eight questions for the factor of values for African centered institutions and cultural expression. The two questions chosen to represent this factor are as follows: The questions were number 20 and 34. Questions #20: Is it intelligent for blacks in America to organize to educate and liberate themselves from white American domination? Questions #34: Should black parents encourage their children to respect all black people good and bad and punish them when they don't show respect?

The 40 respondents had high and low scores of 63 and 34 respectively. Again, the 40 respondents had a lower score over all on the 8 questions that measured the value for African centered institutions and cultural expressions. The African Self Consciousness Scale for the factor was value for African culture. Questions chosen for this factor were questions #5 and #38. Question #5: Should blacks in America try harder to be American than practicing activities that link them up with their African cultural heritage? Question #38: Is the success for an individual black person not as important as the survival of all black people?

The 40 respondents had high and low scores of 40 and 16 respectively. The 40 respondents had overall high scores for this factor of value for African culture. The reader should reference Table 1 for the high and low scores, and the reader can find the questions on the example of the survey at the beginning of the section on quantitative findings.

Table 5 follows the correlation of the four factors in the Baldwin ASCS test

analysis and the five factors or categories of the qualitative analysis from the 10

interviews of elite leadership of the Shrine.

Table 5. Correlations of Four Factors and Qualitative Categories

Factors from Interviews	African Culture	Black Liberation Theology	Black Nationalism	Communalism	Transformation
Baldwin Four Factors	Baldwin Factor I African Identity	Resistant against anti-African forces	African centered institutions and cultural expressions	Value for African culture	Resisting Anti African forces
Response of Survey	F1	F2	F3	F4	
	No. of scores means 93.6	No. of scores mean 66	No of Responses mean 49	No. of Responses Mean 32	ASCS 253.6
	Questions 1-15	Questions 1-11	Questions 1-8	Questions 1-4	
Participant Response	High	High	High	High	

Table 6. Response to Interviews

	Questions
Baldwin Factor 1 Collective African Identity	7. Collective communalism living experience..? 8. Beulah Land 10. How Nguzo Saba relates to the Shrine..?
Baldwin Factor II Resistance to Anti African Forces	4. Black Nationalism 9. Black Consciousness
Baldwin Factor III Value for African Centered Institutions	2. Black Theology 10. Nguzo Saba
Baldwin Factor IV	1. Shrines African Identity

Value for African Culture	7. Collective Communal living
	6. KUA groups

Discussion

The author has participated in numerous activities at the Shrine of the Black

Madonna as a participant observer. The author will begin with the Holocaust Museum.

The feeling received when touring the museum was a shock to the researcher's belief that

Africans had endured slavery without too much pain. However, the researcher was

emotionally disturbed by the MAAFA or the Black Holocaust exhibit. The sign-in sheet

gives a person an opportunity to acknowledge the ancestors by signing one's name and

lighting a candle. The images give the visitor a sense of the horror of slavery. The

Shrine has made the memory of the African enslavement real to whoever visits the

museum. The idea of anti-African forces as one of the factors that Baldwin has used to

identify a trait of the Arocentric personality is made vivid before one's eyes at the

museum.

The Cultural Center at the Shrine is another example of how the Shrine uses

African culture to instill pride in its members. The many masks and artifacts from Africa

give a person a taste for things African in the African personality. The beauty of the

African genius is vivid before the world. The deep reservoir of creative intelligence is

touched by the great works of African artists.

Beulah Land Farm

Beulah Land is 4,000 acres of land bought and owned by the Shrine. The Shrine's members are instilled with the idea that cooperative economics can produce great accomplishments for a people united in their efforts to build lasting institutions that serve African people in the Diaspora. The members talk about the great work they have accomplished through the principles of Kwanzaa and the vision of their leader. The members have constructed numerous buildings on the farm. The researcher visited the farm with members of the Shrine. The researcher could feel the great symbol that Beulah Land represents to all Africans in America. If visitors could only see the vision of the African personality when it recreates the communal values, it would transform our thinking about what blacks can do in the present and future.

History Class

The researcher's experience in the history class that has been offered since June 2009 is highlighted in a ritual of naming a new member. The experience of an African receiving a spear and a new African name was exhilarating and quite informing. The history class and all other events begin with libation to the ancestors. Baldwin lists this as one of the most important African rituals that will restore dignity and render for ancestors. Those ancestors who fought and died for the continuation of African culture and African life are remembered. The history class creates a sense of identity. Some of the subjects are The Early History of Man, The Nile Valley Civilization, The Central African Empires, West African Empires, and the Slave Trade in Africa.

The methodology of the history class is represented as it is in the *Pedagogy of the Oppressed* by Paulo Friere. The class is not traditional; it does not use the Eurocentric methodology of the bank deposit or banking system, where the instructor lectures and deposits knowledge in the student and the student is passive. The banking system treats the student as an inferior and the teacher as superior. In the *Pedagogy of the Oppressed*, the student is equal and he participates in the dialogue with the instructor. There is no master/slave relationship in the class. The student is expected to act on the knowledge given through the dialogue. The class analyzes the history of Africans from the beginning until the present; it also covers Africa and the Diaspora.

The members who participate in the class are active in the community. The factors of Baldwin known as the African Identity and Self-Fortification are incorporated in the people that attend this class. The class is taught from an Afrocentric perspective. The members are instilled with knowledge of their past as Africans acting on the world, knowing their place in world history and the cosmos.

The Worship Service

During the worship service, members feel the energy of each other while they praise God at the Shrine. Musical instruments are played with the usage of drums to bring forth rhythm of the soul and connection with the spirit world they call God. The Cardinal delivers the sermon of the week. The choir sings liberation songs with member participation. Also, baptismal and christening ceremonies are conducted; services always begin with a libation to the ancestor.

Communion

The four principles of communion with God are recited: KutaFutu, FutaMungu, Kuga Sana, and Kugitoa are chanted giving it a spirit of energy emanating from the people. The Shrine uses song and music with a choir and a band. The songs are liberating and the music enchants members to move and participate with everyone. The worship service is where people come to be refueled for the work to be done the next week, month, or year.

The act of doing community work is one of the variables that Baldwin says activates the idea of the Afrocentric personality. The idea of feeding the hungry, clothing the naked, nursing the sick, and caring for the elderly and infants builds the black nation. The many festivals that the Shrine is active in, to name a few, are Malcolm X Day, Marcus Garvey Day, African Liberation Day, and Kwanzaa. There are dances for people of all ages. The Shrine is filled with activities that help create the Afrocentric personality in its members.

Qualitative Study

The five categories used to record the findings in the qualitative interviews are African Culture, Black Liberation Theology, Black Nationalism, Transformation and Communalism. There were ten interviewees from the Shrine leadership.

The first category was African culture. The Nguzo Saba principles created by Maulana Karenga are adopted from African culture. They were used to interpret the responses given by the ten respondents. The principle of self determination was the first principle used in Mwalimu Diallo's responses to the question on self determination. He

stated that the right of Africans to self determination was a God-given right. He also said

that the acquisition of Beulah Land was a collective effort of everyone in the church.

Sister Jaribu defines the Shrine program of incorporation of the two Nguzo Saba

principles of Ujima and Ujamaa which are embedded in the theology of the Shrine. The

principles involve communal work, working together to sustain our own institutions.

Jabari, Chief Administrative office of the Shrine, stated that African culture is expressed

in this statement:

> The Shrine recognizes the person's gift that they bring to the benefit of the
> community. The tradition is that the ancestors begin to consider the person's gift
> when the person is born. They perform a ritual with the elders or doctors where
> they ask the basic question, 'what gift does this person bring the community?'
> The Shrine carries on that same philosophy today.

The Nguzo Saba principle of cooperative economics is adopted from African

culture. Cardinal Mwenda, Brown CEO and Pastor of the Shrine in Atlanta, states that

Beulah Land does this for the community. Beulah Land was acquired in 2000; it is an

idea or process that is portable which can take place in any urban city where there is a

surplus of land. People can cultivate the land, invest in it, and later reap the harvests.

The people can profit from their investment.

The next category that was discussed was the Black Liberation Theology of the

Shrine. The central point in the theology of the Shrine is stated by Mwalimu Diallo. The

theology of the Shrine is that Jesus is the Black Messiah, and even more important is that

Jesus was a revolutionary. Jesus came to liberate the black Nation of Israel and that Jesus

was trying to build an earthly kingdom not a heavenly kingdom. On the question, "How is God represented in the Shrine Theology?," the responses from all ten respondents were that God is a cosmic energy force and creative intelligence means that everything has energy which is a part of God, nature, the earth, the stars, and the universe.

The response of Mwalimu Olatunji to the theology of the Shrine is first that any research reveals that theology itself is the first spiritual teaching which comes out of Africa. It lays the foundation that would later become Christianity, Judaism, and Islam. The Shrine theology is dated by the early writings of the Egyptians or Kemetians where Ptah gives his ideas of ethics in the *Book of the Dead* or *Book of Coming Forth by Day*. All of the major universal religions follow the concepts of MAAT developed by the early African teaching in Kemet. Also the concepts of the Virgin story, the first resurrection story, and the concept of the immaculate conception arise from the story of Osiris, Isis and Heru.

The category of Black Nationalism is best stated by people in the Shrine by the statement by Mwalimu Diallo as the goal of the Shrine. The goal of black nationalism is best described in the book of Rev. Albert Cleage, *Black Christian Nationalism*. He states that BCN would give the black church new direction. The Black Nationalism of BCN is to build a black nation. The black church should be about the business of building the power of God. The Shrine states that if the people are of God's people, then He will be their God, and they will have a covenant with God to build a nation that is heaven on earth.

The idea of communalism is expressed in the intrapersonal relationship between members. The members have meals together and they live together in a communal living environment. They fellowship together and sharing responsibilities for the community. In the teachings of the Shrine, people take care of their fellow man and woman. The effect of communalism on the members is expressed by the relationships between members. The communal living is very effective in bringing people together for a common solution to the problem of people trying to build a nation within a nation. The people share a common experience and common values.

Transformation is the final category and it is the same as salvation. The three processes by which the individual is able to submerge his individualism and become a part of a group experience are stated by Reverend Cleage in the book *Black Christian Nationalism* on page 73. They are (1) the process by which the individual is transformed through a national group experience in which he must face reality, is mirrored in group confrontation, criticism and love; (2) The process by which the individual is transformed through the emotional experience of a rhythmic African religious ceremony deliberately designed to break down the walls of individualism; and (3) the sudden Pentecostal experience which occurs unexpectedly when the walls of individualism have been eroded quietly through sustained, deeply emotional group experiences over an extended period of time.

Mwalimu Diallo's statement in regards to the Shrine programs of transformation is the following. The KUA devotional allows individuals a chance to engage in self-reflection. In order to change one's self and the world, people have to look within themselves to create change. People at the Shrine understand that salvation is a group process and change can come only through groups. Groups such as Al-anon and the

Macabees facilitate change. KUA helps people get in touch with their inner selves so they can move beyond their present state. The transformation that occurs in members in the small KUA group experience produces the people who now have the principle embodied in the African saying, "I am, because we are. We are therefore I am."

Quantitative Study

The quantitative data is an attempt to answer the first research question which is, "does the Shrine produce Afrocentric members with an Afrocentric orientation?" The Afrocentric self consciousness scale test was administered to 40 respondents in the Shrine. The four factors are: (1)the factors of African identity and self fortification, (2) the factor of African resistance to anti African forces, (3) the factor of the value of respondents to Afrocentric institutions and cultural expression, and (4) the factor that pertains to the value for African culture.

The findings for the survey of Baldwin's African self consciousness scale concluded that the 40 respondents scored in the high range for the four factors measured by the instrument. The 40 respondents were on the upper level of the measured factors and had a high range score for overall African self consciousness. The 40 respondents had a high degree of African centered consciousness. The personalities of the 40 respondents as measured by the survey shows that they are highly Afrocentric. The survey clearly indicates that the 40 respondents were conscious of their African centered program in the Shrine of the Black Madonna, as indicated by the qualitative survey and the five categories derived from the surveys.

The African Self-Consciousness Scale Survey

INSTRUCTIONS: The following statements reflect some beliefs, opinions and attitudes of Black people. Read each statement carefully and give your honest feelings about the beliefs and attitudes expressed. Indicate the extent to which you agree or disagree using the following scale.

1 = Very strongly Disagree   2 = Strongly Disagree   3 = Moderately Disagree

4 = Slightly Disagree   5 = Slightly Agree   6 = Moderately Agree

7 = Strongly Agree   8 = Very Strongly Agree

Note that the higher the number you choose for the statement, the more you <u>Agree</u> with that statement; and conversely, the lower the number you choose, the more you <u>Disagree</u> with that statement. Also, there are no right or wrong answers, only the answer that best expresses your present feelings about the statement. Please respond to **ALL** of the statement (do not omit any). <u>Bubble-in your choices in the space provided.</u>

ANSWER CHOICES – PLEASE CHOOSE ONLY ONE	1	2	3	4	5	6	7	8
1. I do not necessarily feel like I am being mistreated in a situation where I see another Black person being mistreated.	0	0	0	0	0	0	0	0
2. Black people should have their own independent schools, which consider their African heritage and values an important part of the curriculum.	0	0	0	0	0	0	0	0
3. Blacks who trust Whites in general are basically very intelligent beings.	0	0	0	0	0	0	0	0
4. Blacks who are committed and prepared to uplift the (Black) race by any means necessary (including violence) are more intelligent than Blacks who are not this committed and prepared.	0	0	0	0	0	0	0	0
5. Blacks in America should try harder to be American than practicing activities that link them up with their African cultural heritage.	0	0	0	0	0	0	0	0
6. Regardless of their interests, educational background and social achievements, I would prefer to associate with Black people than with non-Blacks.	0	0	0	0	0	0	0	0
7. It is not a good idea for Black students to be required to learn an African language.	0	0	0	0	0	0	0	0
8. It is not within the best interest of Blacks to depend on Whites for anything, no matter how religious and decent they (the Whites) purport to be.	0	0	0	0	0	0	0	0
9. Blacks who place the highest value on Black life (over that of other people) are reverse racists and generally evil people.	0	0	0	0	0	0	0	0
10. Black children should be taught that they are African people at an early age.	0	0	0	0	0	0	0	0

ANSWER CHOICES – PLEASE CHOOSE ONLY ONE	1	2	3	4	5	6	7	8
11. White people, generally speaking, are not opposed to self-determination for Blacks.	0	0	0	0	0	0	0	0
12. As a good index of self-respect, Blacks in America should consider adopting traditional African names for themselves.	0	0	0	0	0	0	0	0
13. A White/European or Caucasian image of God and the "holy family" (among others considered close to God) are not such bad things for Blacks to worship.	0	0	0	0	0	0	0	0
14. Blacks born in the United States are Black or African first, rather than American of just plain people.	0	0	0	0	0	0	0	0
15. Black people who talk in a relatively loud manner, show a lot of emotions and feelings, and express themselves with a lot of movement and body motion are less intelligent than Blacks who do not behave this way.	0	0	0	0	0	0	0	0
16. Racial consciousness and cultural awareness based on traditional African values are necessary to the development of Black marriages and families that can contribute to the liberation and enhancement of Black people in America.	0	0	0	0	0	0	0	0
17. In dealing with other Blacks, I consider myself quite different and unique from most of them.	0	0	0	0	0	0	0	0
18. Blacks should form loving relationships and marry only other Blacks.	0	0	0	0	0	0	0	0
19. I have difficulty identifying with the culture of African People.	0	0	0	0	0	0	0	0
20. It is intelligent for Blacks in America to organize to educate and liberate themselves form White-American domination.	0	0	0	0	0	0	0	0
21. There is no such thing as African culture among Blacks in America.	0	0	0	0	0	0	0	0
22. It is good for Black husbands and wives to help each other develop racial consciousness and cultural awareness in themselves and their	0	0	0	0	0	0	0	0
23. Africa is not the ancestral homeland of all Black people throughout the world.	0	0	0	0	0	0	0	0
24. It is good for Blacks in America to wear traditional African-type clothing and hairstyles if they desire to do so.	0	0	0	0	0	0	0	0

ANSWER CHOICES – PLEASE CHOOSE ONLY ONE	1	2	3	4	5	6	7	8
25. I feel little sense of commitment to Black people who are not close friends or relatives.	0	0	0	0	0	0	0	0
26. All Black students in Africa and America should be expected to study African culture and history as it occurs throughout the world.	0	0	0	0	0	0	0	0
27. Black children should be taught to love all races of people, even those races who do harm to them.	0	0	0	0	0	0	0	0
28. Blacks in America who view Africa as their homeland are more intelligent than those who view America as their homeland.	0	0	0	0	0	0	0	0
29. If I saw Black children fighting, then I would leave them to settle it alone.	0	0	0	0	0	0	0	0
30. White people, generally speaking, do not respect Black life.	0	0	0	0	0	0	0	0
31. Blacks in America should view Blacks from other countries (e.g., Ghana, Nigeria and other countries in Africa) as foreigners rather than as their brothers and sisters.	0	0	0	0	0	0	0	0
32. When a Black person uses the terms, "Self, Me and I," his/her reference should encompass all Black people rather than simply her/himrself.	0	0	0	0	0	0	0	0
33. Religion is dangerous for Black people when it directs and inspires them to become self-determining and independent of the White community.	0	0	0	0	0	0	0	0
34. Black parents should encourage their children to respect all Black people, good and bad, and punish them when they don't show respect.	0	0	0	0	0	0	0	0
35. Blacks who celebrate Kwanzaa and practice the "Nguzo Saba" (the Black Value System), both symbolizing African traditions, don't necessarily have better sense than Blacks who celebrate Easter.	0	0	0	0	0	0	0	0
36. African culture is better for humanity than European culture.	0	0	0	0	0	0	0	0
37. Black people's concern for self-knowledge (knowledge of one's history, philosophy, culture, etc.) and self (collective) determination makes them treat White people badly.	0	0	0	0	0	0	0	0
38. The success of an individual Black person is not as important as the survival of all Black people.	0	0	0	0	0	0	0	0
39. If a good/worthwhile education could be obtained at all schools (both Black and White), I would prefer for my child to attend a racially integrated school.	0	0	0	0	0	0	0	0

ANSWER CHOICES – PLEASE CHOOSE ONLY ONE	1	2	3	4	5	6	7	8
40. It is good for Black people to refer to each other as brother and sister because such practice is consistent with our African heritage.	0	0	0	0	0	0	0	0
41. It is not necessary to require Black/African studies courses in predominantly Black schools.	0	0	0	0	0	0	0	0
42. Being involved in wholesome group activities with other Blacks lifts my spirits more so than being involved in individual oriented activities.	0	0	0	0	0	0	0	0

CHAPTER V

CONCLUSION

This study of the Shrine of the Black Madonna has employed two models of how Africans can proceed in nation building as presented by Baldwin in his book, *African Black Psychology in the American Context*. The Shrine of the Black Madonna and the Afrocentric personality was evaluated on the building of the African personality and the processes of creating an African national consciousness. In this study, the Shrine has stated that the liberation of African people is sacred. The Shrine has begun the process of African reaffirmation through its education of Africans and in its usage of black history and African culture for the revival of the community of the African world from antiquity to the present with emphasis on Nubian and Kemetian high culture.

The model presented by Kwame Aggei Akoto in his book, *African Nation Building* is called a model of re-Africanization. The renewal of national and cultural consciousness is defined as a new reality for African people. This renewed African centered reality marks the rebirth of the African personality and revitalization of African nationality. Akoto identified three stages of re-Africanization: (1) Rediscovery /Historical Recovery, (2) Redefinition/Cultural Re-affirmation, and (3) Revitalization/National Liberation.

The Shrine of the Black Madonna represents all three stages in its black Christian nationalist practices. The uses of black history classes to teach its members the true history of African people is the foundation upon which the Shrine builds the new Afrocentric personality. Akoto states, "The systematic exhumation and revivification of African history throughout the continent and the Diaspora from antiquity to the present."[1] The Shrine has begun this process by establishing shrines in Liberia and Ghana. The Pan African Nationalism of the Shrine represents a rebirth of African cooperation in terms of political, economic and cultural alliances.

The first stage of rediscovery and historical recovery includes the recovering and revitalization of the core values of African antiquity. The sacred works, philosophy, languages, and other symbolic forms and re-linking of the vital Kushitic and Kemetian civilization must be recovered. Also, people must rediscover the traditional African societies that have survived in present-day Africa.

Akoto states, "history is culture and culture is history."[2] The second stage of redefinition and cultural reaffirmation must involve the remaking of an African centered evaluation of those positive values and behaviors that have developed from our adaptation to and participation in the contemporary life of the world. Akoto sees the utilization of Pan African nationalism and the development of Pan African nationalist institutional infrastructure, including education, defense, and industrial development as critical to the African centered redefinition and cultural reaffirmation process.

---

1. K. A. Akoto, *Nation Building: Theory and Practice of African Centered Education*, (Washington, DC: Pan African World Institute, 1992), 6.

2. Ibid., 7.

The Shrine of the Black Madonna has begun this process through the five categories the researcher believed are represented in the qualitative section of this research. The five categories are African Culture, Black Liberation Theology, Black Nationalism, Transformation, and Communalism. The first category is African Culture. The Nguzo Saba principles created by Maulana Karenga are adapted to identify how the Shrine uses African values to build the black nation's consciousness. The economic development of the nation is demonstrated in the Shrine's maintenance of the Beulah Land Farms. The Shrine, as shown in the researcher's discussion of the principles of the Nguzo Saba in Chapter Four of this dissertation, indicates that the Shrine has revived the core values of African culture. The black liberation theology of the Shrine redefines Christianity and uses it as a tool to liberate the mind of Africans in America.

The Shrine's use of communalism is practiced by its members in its relationships with the idea of collective identity and sharing with each other. The common living arrangements of the members further their understanding of communal values. The third stage of Akoto's plan is revitalization and national liberation. The emphasis is on the fusion or synthesis of a traditional African cultural infrastructure. Also, principles and practices and contemporary Pan African nationalism, along with those culturally compatible aspects of modern technology are important.[3]

The Shrine of the Black Madonna has practiced the ideas stated by Akoto in their programs of liberation of the black nation. In the quantitative section of this dissertation, the researcher presents the four principles stated by Joseph Baldwin. The four factors stated are:

---

3. Ibid., 8.

1. The factors of African Identity and self-fortification.

2. The factor of African resistance to anti-African forces.

3. The factor of the value of respondents to Afrocentric institutions and cultural expressions.

4. The factor that pertains to the value of African Culture.

These factors are shown to be highly stable in the members of the Shrine of the Black Madonna as reflected in the high scores on the Baldwin Personality Scale Test in Chapter IV of this project. Kambon's (a.k.a. Joseph Baldwin) model of African reclamation and re-Africanization states:

1. Through massive reeducation of the African community in America and throughout the world we must develop a Pan-African Nationalist consciousness and identity.

2. The African community in America must establish an African identity reclamation rite which allows for a formal process/ritual of conscious cultural identity. (Pan African National Consciousness)

3. The African community in America and throughout the world must reject and relinquish (both symbolically and in actuality) any connection of non-African to African reality, especially European and Eurasian culture.

4. The African community must return to a belief in and practice of traditional African-centered cosmology, cosmogony, ontology, and spiritualism linked chronologically to the Pan-African present (i.e., informed by cumulative historical African experience and wisdom as the center of African reality).[4]

The way Africans in America and Africans throughout the world can accomplish these objectives that Kambon has proposed is to begin to practice the ideas incorporated in the program of the Black Madonna organization. However, the Shrine of the Black Madonna

---

4. Kobi K. K. Kambon, *The African Black Psychology in the American Context: An African-Centered Approach* (Tallahassee, FL: Nubian Nation Publican, 1998), 447-457.

has done most, if not all, of the four things Kambon states as a condition for beginning the process. The four things that must be done to set forth a victorious thrust are:

1. Africans must give back European and Eurasian enemies of Africa their Gods.

2. Africans must give back the European and Eurasian enemies of Africa their languages.

3. Africans must give back European and Eurasian enemies of Africa their names.

4. Africans must give back European and Eurasian enemies of Africa their cultural beliefs and values, customs and rituals.[5]

These ideas of Kambon are some of the ideas incorporated in the teachings of Reverend Albert Cleage. The Shrine of the Black Madonna has produced Africans with Afrocentric personality as shown in this study. The Afrocentric personality of the Shrine members is reflected in their marriage ceremony where not only do mates marry each other, but their union serves a higher purpose—that is, the liberation of Africans on planet earth.

The Shrine of the Black Madonna definitely produces members with an Afrocentric personality. The transformation of members occurs during the KUA group sessions. The use of Afrcocentric symbols and activities reinforce the members' new worldview. The researcher recommends that others study other organizations that create an African centered program such as the Nation of Islam, the US Organization, and the Hebrew Israelites. There are similarities in their programs. The emphasis on African culture is the key to the development of a Pan-African consciousness in Africa and African people in the Diaspora. There should be a concerted effort by Africans to

---

5. Ibid., 454-455.

understand and use the principles and lessons of the indigenous African culture on the continent of Africa. The ideology of Pan-Africanism should proceed from reclamation of African history and culture. Our ideology should include extensive research of Kemet. Kemet is our classical civilization and it still lives in the many villages and societies of present day Africa.

APPENDIX

Raw Scores ASCS Test and Field Notes

Factor 1 Collective African Identity and Self-Fortification

Item: 1,2,4,6,10,12,14,16,15,23,26,30,36,40,42 (15 items)
Score: 106/120 High Range

1=7, 2=8, 3=8, 4=5, 6=8 ,8=1, 9=8, 10=8, 11=6, 12=7 ,13=4, 14=7
15=6, 16=8, 18=7, 20=8, 23=8,20=8,
30=7, 36=6, 40=6, 42=8

Factor II Resistance Against Anti-African Force

Items: 3,8,9,13,15,17,3,1,33,37,41 (11 items)
Total Score: 64 = High Range 64/88
High Range 55.5-88

3=8 ,8=8, 9=8, 13=5, 15=3, 17=2, 31=7, 33=8, 37=8, 41=7

Factor III Value for African-Centered Institutions and Cultural Expressions

Items: 20,22,24,25,27,29,34,39 (8 items)
Total Score: 51 /64 High Value

20=8, 22=8, 24=7, 25=7, 27=1, 29=8, 34=6, 39=6

Factor IV Value for African-Centered Institutions and Cultural Expressions

Items: 5, 7, 19, 21, 28 (5 items)
Total Score: 42 42/336 High

5=8, 7=8, 19=8, 21=7, 28=4

ASCS Score 256/336
Score 35/40
35 High Value

#2

Factor I Collective African Identity and Self-Fortification

Items: 1,2,4,6,10,12,14,16,18,23,26,30,36,40,42,(15 items)
Score Total: 112
High Range
112/120

1=8, 2=8, 4=7, 6=8, 10=8, 12=8, 14=5, 16=6, 18=7, 23=8,
 26=8, 30=8, 36=8, 40=8, 42=7

Factor II Resistance Against Anti-African Forces

Items: 3,8,9,13,15,17,31,32,33,37,41 (11 items)
Score: 72/88
High Range: 55.5/88

3=8, 8=5, 9=8, 13=8, 15=8, 17=4, 31=8, 32=8, 33=1, 37=6, 41=8

Factor III Value for African-Centered Institution and Cultural Expressions

Items: 20,22,24,25,27,29,34,39 (8 items)
Total: 61   61/64
High Range 40.5/64

20=8, 22=8, 24=8, 25=8, 27=7, 29=7, 34=7, 39=8

Factor IV Value for African-Centered Institutions and Cultural Expressions

Items: 5,7,19,21,28 (5 items)
Total: 40
High Range 40/40
289/336 High ASCS

5=7, 7=8, 19=8, 21=8, 28=8

#3
Factor I Collective African Identity and Self-Fortification

Items: 1,2,4,6,10,12,16,18,23,26,30,36,40,42 (14 items)
Total: 108/120
High Range 75.5/120

1=7, 2=8, 4=6, 6=5, 10=8, 12=7, 16=8, 18=4, 23=8, 26=8, 30=7, 36=8, 40=8, 42=8

Factor II Resistance Against Anti-African Forces

Items: 3,8,9,13,15,17,31,32,33,37,41 (11 items)
Total Score: 70/88
High Range 70/88
55.8/88

3=4, 8=8, 9=8, 13=8, 15=1, 17=4, 31=8, 32=5, 33=8, 37=8, 41=8

Factor III Value for African-Centered Institutions and Cultural Expressions

Items: 20,22,24,25,27,29,34,39 (8 items)
Total Score: 52
High Range

20=8, 22=8, 24=8, 25=8, 27=5, 29=4, 34=7, 39=4

Factor IV Value for African-Centered Institutions and Cultural Expressions

Items: 5,7,19,21,28 (5 items)
Total Score: 36/40
High Range

5=8, 7=8, 19=8, 21=4, 28=8

ASCS Score: 2366/336
High ASCS Score: 252/336

#4

Factor I Collective African Identity and Self-Fortification

Items: 5,1,2,3,6,10,12,14,16,18,23,26,30,36,40,42 (15 items)
Total Score: 120/120
High ASCS 75.5/120

1=8, 2=8, 4=8, 6=8, 10=8, 12=8, 14=8, 16=8, 18=8, 23=8,
 26=8, 30=8, 36=8, 40=8, 42=8

Factor II Resistance Against Anti-African Forces

Items: 3,8,9,13,15,17,31,32,33,37,39 (11 items)
Total Score: 78 78/88
High Range: 55.5/88

3=8, 8=8, 9=8, 13=8, 15=3, 17=6, 31=8, 31=8, 32=5, 33=8, 37=8, 41=8

Factor III Value for African-Centered Institutions and Cultural Expressions

Items: 20.22,24,25,27,29,34,39 (8 items)
Total Score: 61   62/64
High Range
40.5/64

20=8, 22=8, 24=8, 25=6, 27=8, 29=8, 34=7, 39=8

Factor IV Value for African-Centered Institutions and Cultural Expressions

Items: 5,7,19,21,28 (5 items)
Total Score: 40
40/40 High Range

5=8, 7=8, 19=8, 21=8, 28=8

Total ASCS 299/336
High ASCS 252/336

#5
Factor I Collective African Identity and Self-Fortification

Items: 1,2,4,6,10,12,14,16,18,23,26,30,36,40,42 (15 items)
Total Score: 88
High Score: 88/120
High Range: 75.5/120

1=6, 2=7, 4=1, 6=3, 10=8, 12=8, 14=8, 16=8, 18=6,
 23=8, 26=8, 30=3, 36=8, 40=6, 42=8

Factor II Resistance Against Anti-African Forces

Items: 3,8,9,13,15,17,31,32,37,41
Total Score: 60/88
High Range : 55.5/88

3=6, 8=1, 9=8, 13=8,15=8, 17=8, 31=8, 32=8, 37=8, 41=8

Factor III Value for African-Centered Institutions and Cultural Expressions

Items: 20, 22,24,25,27,29,34,36
Total Score: 44/64
High Range
Total Score 34/40
High Range

20-8, 22=8, 24=8, 258, 27=8, 29=8

Factor IV Value for African-Centered Institutions and Cultural Expressions

Items: 5,7,19,21,28 (5 items)
Total Score: 34/40
High Range
 5=8, 7=8, 19=8, 21=8, 28=2

Total Overall Score 226/336
Middle Range: 121/256

#6

Factor 1 Collective African Identity and Self-Fortification

Items: 1,2,4,6,10,12,14,16,18,23,26,30,36,40,42
Total Score: 105/120
High Range
75.5/120

1=8, 2=8, 4=7, 6=5, 10=8, 12=6, 14=8, 16=8. 18=6,
23=8, 26=8, 30=6, 36=6, 40=7, 42=6

Factor II Resistance Against Anti-African Forces

Items: 3,8,9,13,15,17,31,32,33,37,41 (11 items)
Total Score: 79/88
High Range
55.5/88

3=5, 8=8, 9=8,13=8, 15=7, 17=4, 31=8, 32=7, 33=8, 37=8, 41=8

Factor III Value for African-Centered Institutions and Cultural Expressions

Items: 20,22,24,25,27,29,34,39 (8 items)
Total Score: 56/64
High Range
40.5/64

20=8, 22=8, 24=8, 25=8, 27=4, 29=7, 34=8, 39=5

Factor IV Value for Africa-Centered Institutions and Cultural Expressions

Items: 5,7,19,27,28 (5 items)
Total Score: 32/40
High Range

5=7, 7=7, 19=8, 21=5, 28=5

Total Score Overall ASCS 272/336
High Range 252/336

#7

Factor Collective African Identity and Self-Fortification

Items: 1,2,4,6,10,12,14,16,18,23,26,30,36,40,42 (15 items)
Total Score: 99/120
High Range

1=5, 2=8, 4=3, 6=4, 10=8, 12=8, 14=6, 16=8,
18=8, 23=7, 26=5, 30=6, 36=7, 40=8, 42=8

Factor II Resistance Against Anti-African Forces

Items: 3,8,19,13,15,17,31,32,33,37,41 (11 items)
Total Score: 81/88
High Range 55.5/88

3=8, 8=7, 9=8, 13=8, 15=8, 17=8, 31=7, 32=4, 33=8, 37=8, 41=7

Factor III Value for African-Centered Institutions and Cultural Expressions

Items: 20,22,24,25,27,29,34,39 (8 items)
Total Score: 46/64
High Range
40.5/ 64

20=8, 22=8, 24=7, 15=6, 17=7, 29=8, 34=5, 39=6

Factor IV Value for African-Centered Institutions and Cultural Expressions

Items: 5,7,19,21,28 (5 items)
Total Score: 25/40
High Range

5=8, 7=5, 19=4, 21=3, 28=5

Total Score Overall 252/336 Range
ASCS High Score Range 252/336

#8

Factor I, Collective African Identity and Self-Fortification

Items: 1,2,4,6,10,m12,14,16,18,2326,30,36,40,42 (15 items)
Total Score: 103/120
High Range 75.5/120

1=7, 2=7, 4=5, 6=6, 10=8, 12=6, 14=7, 16=8, 18=5, 232=8, 26=6, 30-8, 36=7 40=7, 42=8

Factor II Resistance Against Anti-African Forces

Items: 3,8,9,13,15,17,31,32,33,37,41 (11 items)
Total Score: 59/88
High Range
55.5/88

3=6, 8=5, 9=3, 13=7, 15=5, 17=6, 31=7, 32=7, 33=1, 37=7, 41=6

Factor III Value for African-Centered Institutions and Cultural Expressions

Items: 20,22,24,25,27,29,34,39 (8 items)
Total Score: 46/64
High Range
40.5/64

20=8, 22=7, 24=6, 25=6, 27=5, 29=7, 34=6, 39=1

Factor IV Value for African-Centered Institutions and Cultural Expressions

Items: 5,7,19,21,28 (5 items)
Total Score: 31/40
High Range 20.5/40

5=7, 7=6, 19=7, 21=7, 28=4

Total Score Overall 239/336

#9

Factor I Collective African Identity and Self-Fortification

Items: 1,2,4,6,10,12,14,16,18,23,26,30,36,40,42 (15 items)
Total Score: 114/120
High Range
75.5/120

1=7, 2=8, 4=5, 6=8, 10=8, 12=8, 14=8, 16=8,18=7, 23=8, 26=8, 30=7, 36=8, 40=8, 42=8

Factor III Resistance Against African forces

Items: 3,8,9,13,15,17,31,32,33,37,41 (11 items)
Total Score: 81/88
High Range
55.5/88

3=7, 8=7, 9=8, 13=8, 15=8, 17=7, 31=8, 32=4, 33=8, 37=8, 41=8

Factor III Value for African-Centered Institution and Cultural Expressions

Items: 5,20,22,24,25,27,29,34,39 (8 items)
Total Score 59/64
High Range40.5/64

20=8, 22=8, 24-8, 26=8, 27=5, 29=7, 34=7, 39=8

Factor IV Value for African-Centered Institutions and Cultural Expressions

Items: 5,7,19,21,28 (5 items)
Total Score: 38/40
High Range20.5/40

5=8, 7=8, 19=8, 21=8, 28=6

Total Score Overall ASCS: 292/336
High Range ASCS: 252/336

#10

Factor I Collective African Identity and Self-Fortification

Items: 1,2,4,6,10,12,14,16,18,23,26,30,36,40,42 (15 items)
Total Score: 115/120
High Range
Total Overall Score   293/336 High ASCS Score

1=7, 2=8, 4=5, 6=8, 10=8, 12=8, 14=8, 16=8. 18=8, 23=8, 26=8, 30=7, 36=8, 40=8, 42=8

Factor II Resistance Against Anti-African Forces

Items: 3,8,9,13,15,17,31,32,33, 37,41 (11items)
Total Score: 82/88
High Range

3=7, 8=7, 9=8, 13=8, 15=8, 17=7, 31=8, 32=5, 33=8, 38=8, 41=8

Factor III Value for African-Centered Institutions and Cultural Expression

Items: 20,22,24,25,27,29,34,39 (8 items)
Total Score: 58/64
High Range

20=8, 22=8, 24=8, 25=8, 27=4, 29=7, 34=7, 39=8

Factor IV Value for African-Centered Institutions and Cultural Expressions

Items: 5,7,19,21,28 (5 items)
Total Score: 38/40

5=8, 7=8, 19=8, 21=8, 28=6

Total Overall Score ASCS   293/336
High ASCS Score Range 252/336

#11

Factor I Collective African Identity and Self-Fortification

Items: 1,2,4,6,10,12,14,16,18,23,26,30,36,40,42 (15 items)
Total Score: 105/120
High Range 75.5/120

1=8, 2=7, 4=5, 6=8, 10=8, 12=5, 14=8, 16=8, 18=4, 23=8, 26=8, 30=6, 36=6, 40=8, 42=8

Factor II Resistance Against Anti-African Forces

Items: 3,8,9,13,15,17,31,32,33,37,41 (11 items)
Total Score: 75/88
High Range: 55/5/88

3=8, 8=6, 9=8, 13=8, 15=8, 17=8, 31=8, 32=1, 33=8, 37=8, 41=8

Factor III Value for African-Centered Institutions and Cultural Expressions

Items: 20,22,24,25,27,29,34,39 (8 items)
Total Score: 43/64
High Range: 40.5/64

20=8, 22=8, 24=8, 25=1, 17=1, 29=8, 34=1, 39=8

Factor IV Value for African-Centered Institutions and Cultural Expressions

Items: 5,7,19,21,28 (5 items)
Total Score: 35/40
High Range

5=8, 7==8, 19=8, 21=8, 28=3

Total Overall Score ASCS: 258/336
High ASCS Score Range: 252/336

#12

Factor I Collective African Identity and Self-Fortification

Items: 1,2,4,6,10,12,14,16,18,23,26,30,36,40,42 (15 items)
Total Score: 73/120
Low Range: 15/75

1=7, 2=3, 4=1, 6=6, 10=8, 12=3, 14=5, 16=2, 18=6, 23=8, 26=6, 30=5, 36=4, 40=5, 42=4

Factor II Resistance Against Anti-African Forces

Items: 3,8,9,13,15,17,31,32,33,37,41 (11 items)
Total Score: 62/88
High Range: 55:5/88

3=8, 8=5, 9=7, 13=8, 15=4, 17=5, 31=6, 32=1, 33=8, 37=7, 41=3

Factor III Value for African-Centered Institution and Cultural Expressions

Items: 20,22,24,25,27,29,34,39 (8 items)
Total Score: 36/64
Low Range: 8/40

20-4, 22=6, 24=7, 25=3, 27=4, 29=6, 34=2, 39=4

Factor IV Value for African-Centered Institutions and Cultural Expressions

Items: 5,7,19,21,28 (5 items)
Total Score: 26/40
High Range: 20.5/40

5=5, 7=4, 9=7, 21=7, 28=3

Total Overall Score ASCS: 197/336
Middle Range ASCS: 127/251

#13

Factor I Collective African Identity and Self-Fortification

Items: 1,2,4,6,10,12,14,16,18,23,26,20,26,40,42 (15 items)
Total Score: 98/120
High Range: 75.5/120

1=8, 2=1, 4=6, 10=8, 12=8, 14=8, 16=8, 18=8, 23=2, 26=7, 30=8, 36=8, 40=8, 42=8

Factor II Resistance Against Anti-African Forces

Items: 3,8,9,13,15,17,31,32,33,37,41 (11 items)
Total Store: 66/88
High Range: 55.5/88

3=1, 8=6, 9=8, 13=8, 15=5, 17=6, 31=8, 32=8, 33=8, 37=7, 41=1

Factor III Value for African-Centered Institutions and Cultural Expressions

Items: 20,22,24,25,27,29,34,39 (8 items)
Tot Score: 49/64
High Range: 40.5/64

20=8, 22=8, 24=7, 25=2, 27=7, 29=2, 34=8, 39=7

Factor IV Value for African Institutions and Cultural Expressions

Items: 5,7,19,21,28 (5 items)
Total Score: 26/40
High Range: 20.5/40

5=1, 7=1, 19=8, 21=8, 28=8

Total Score Overall: 239/336
Middle Range ASCS Score:127/251

#14

Factor I, Collective African Identity and Self-Fortification

Items: 1,2,4,6,10,12,14,16,18,23,26,30,36,40,42 (11 items)
Total Score: 101/120
High Range: 75.5/120

1=5, 2=8, 4=4, 6=8, 10=7, 12=8, 14=8, 16=8, 18=8,23=3, 26=8, 30=8. 36=8, 40=8 42=2

Factor II, Resistance Against Anti-African Forces

Items: 3,8,9,13,15,17,31,32,33,37,40 (11 items)
Total Score: 35///88
Low Range: 15/55

3=8, 8=3, 9=4, 13=2, 15=1, 17=4, 321=1, 32=8, 33=2, 37=1, 40=1

Factor III Value for African-Centered Institution and Cultural Expressions

Items: 20,22,24,25,27,29,34,39 (8 items)
Total Score: 40
High Range: 40/64

20-7, 22-7, 24=8, 25=1, 27=2, 29=7, 34=7, 39=1

Factor IV Value for African-Centered Institutions and Cultural Expressions

Items: 5,7,19,21,28 (5 items)
Total Score: 16
Low Range: 16/40

5=1, 7=1, 19=1, 21=7, 28=6

#15

Factor I Collective African Identity and Self-Fortification

Items: 1,2,4,6,10,12,14,16,18,23,26,30,36,40,42 (15 items)
Total Score: 57/120
Low Range 15/75

1=4, 2=1, 4=1, 6=5, 10=1, 12=2, 14=1, 16=1, 18=1, 23=8, 26=5, 30=6, 36=8, 40=5, 42=8

Factor II Resistance Against Anti-African Forces

Items: 3,8,9,3,15,17,31,32,33,37,41 (11 items)
Total Score: 43/64
High Range: 40.5/64

20=5, 22=8, 24=1, 25=8, 27=5, 29=8, 34=1, 39=7

Factor IV Value for African-Centered Institutions and Cultural Expressions

Items: 5,7,19,21,28 (5 items)

5=4, 7=8, 19=8, 21=8, 28=2

#16

Factor I Collective African Identity and Self-Fortification

Item: 1,2,4,6,10,12,16,18,23,26,30,36,40,42 (15 items)
Total Score: 93/120
High Range: 75.5/120

1=8, 2=6, 4=4, 6=7, 10=7, 12=7, 16=7, 18=7, 23=8, 26=7, 30=6, 40=8, 42=6

Factor II Resistance Against Anti-African Forces

Items: 3,8,9,13,15,17,31,32,33,37,41 (11 items)
Total Score: 77/88
High Range: 55.5/88

3=7, 8=8, 9=7, 13=8, 15=6, 17=7, 31=7, 32=4, 33=8, 37=8, 41=7

Factor III Value for African-Centered Institutions and Cultural Expressions

Items: 20,22,24,25,27,29,34,39 (8 items)
Total Score: 53/64
High Range: 40.5/64

20=8, 22=7, 24=7, 25=7, 27=6, 29=6, 34=5, 39=7

Factor IV Value for African-Centered Institutions and Cultural Expressions

Items: 5,7,19,21,28 (5 items) Total Score: 36/40
High Range: 20.5/40
Total Score Overall: 259/336
High Range: 251/336

5=8, 7=7, 19=7, 21=7, 28=7

#17
Factor I Collective African Identity and Self-Fortification

Items: 1,2,4,6,10,12,14,16,18,23,26,30,36,40,42
Total Score: 96/120
High Range: 75.5/120

1=7, 2=7, 4=2, 6=7, 10=8, 12=6, 14=8, 16=7, 18=6, 23=8, 26=4, 30=7, 36=4, 40=7,
42=8

Factor II Resistance Against Anti-African Forces

Items: 3,8,9,13,15,17,31,32,33,37,41 (11 items)
Total Score: 54/88
Low Range: 11/55

3=4, 8=8, 9=4, 13=3, 15=4, 17=5, 31=7, 32=5, 33=4, 37=5, 41=5

Factor III Value for African-Centered Institutions and Cultural Expressions

Items: 20,22,24,25,27,29,34,39 (8 items)
Total Score: 46/64
High Range: 40.5/64

20=7, 22=7, 24=5, 25=6, 27==4, 29=7, 34=7, 39=3

Factor IV Value for African-Centered Institutions and Cultural Expressions

Items: 5,7,19,21,28 (5 items)
Total Score: 35/40
High Range: 20.5/40
Total Overall Score ASCS
231/336
Middle Range ASCS: 127/251

5=8, 7=7, 19=8, 21=7, 28=5

#18

Factor I Collective African Identity and Self-Fortification

Items: 1,2,4,6,10,12,14,16,18,23,26,30,36,40,42
Total Score: 68/120
Low Range

1=7, 2=4, 6=4, 10=4, 12=3, 14=4, 16=4, 18=4, 23=5, 26=5, 30=6, 36=5, 40=3, 42=5

Factor II Resistance Against Anti-African Forces

Items: 3,8,9,13,15,17,31,32,33,37,41 (11 items)
Total Score: 52/88
Low Range: 11/55

3=7, 8=1, 9=6, 13=5, 15=5, 17=5, 31=5, 32=5, 33=5, 37=5, 41=3

Factor III Value for African-Centered Institutions and Cultural Expression

Items: 20,22,24,25,27,29,34,39 (8 items)
Total Score: 4-/64
High Range: 40/64

20=4m 22-6m 24-4m 25=5, 27=5, 29=8, 34=5, 39=4

Factor IV Value for African-Centered Institutions and Cultural Expressions

Items: 5,7,19,21,28 (5 items)
Total Score: 36/40
High Range Score Overall ASCA
Total Score Middle Range 196/336

5=8, 7=8, 19=5, 21=7, 28=8

Total Score ASCS
Middle Range: 1296/336
Middle Range 127/251

#19

Factor I Collective African Identity and Self-Fortification

Items: 1,2,4,6,10,12,14,16,18,23,26,30,36,41,42
Total Score: 109/120
High Range ASCS

1=7, 2=8, 4=6, 6=6, 10=8. 12=7. 14=7, 16=8, 23=8
26=8, 30=5, 36=8, 40=8,42=8

Factor II Resistance Against Anti-African Forces

Items: 3,7,9,13,15,17,31,32,22,27,41 (11 items)
Total Score: 77/88
High Range ASCS

3=7, 8=1, 9=8, 13=8, 15=8, 17=8, 31=8, 33=8, 37=8, 41=8

Factor III Value for African-Centered Institutions and Cultural Expression

Items: 20,22,24,25,27,29,34,39 (8 items)
Total Score: 56/64
High Range Score

20=8, 22=8, 24=8, 25=8, 27=6, 29=8, 34=6, 30=4

Factor IV Value for African Institutions and Cultural Expressions

Items: 5,7,19,21,28 (5 items)
Total Score: 28/40
High Range
Overall 270/336 High

5=8, 7=2, 19=8, 21=6, 28=4

#20

Factor I Collective African Identity and Self-Fortification

Items: 1,2,4,6,10,12,14,16,18,23,26,30,36,40,42 (15 items)
Total Score: 102/120
High Range

1=2, 2=8, 4=2, 6=7, 10=7, 12=5, 14=7, 16=8, 18=8, 23=8, 26=8, 30=8, 36=8, 40=8, 42=8

Factor II Resistance Against Anti-African Forces

Items: 3,8,9,13,15,17,31,32,33,37,41 (11 items)
Total Score: 80/88
High Range

3=8, 8=6, 9=8, 15=8, 17=2, 31=8, 33=8, 37=8, 41=8

Factor III Value for African-Centered Institutions and Cultural Expressions

Items: 20,22,24,25,27,29,34,39 (8 items)
Total Score: 57/64
High Range

20=8, 22-8, 24=4, 25=8, 27=7, 29=8, 34=6, 39=8

Factor IV Value for African-Centered Institutions and Cultural Expressions

Items: 5,7,19,21,28 (5 items)
Total Score: 30/40
High Range

5=1, 7=6, 19=8, 21=8, 28=7

Total Overall ASCS
269/336
High ASCS Score Range

#21

Factor I Collective African Identity and Self-Fortification

Items: 1,2,4,6,10,12,14,16,18,23,26,30,36,40,42 (15 items)
Total Score: 73/120
Low Range
Middle Range: 199/336 ASCS

1=3, 2=5, 4=3, 6=6, 10=6, 12=3, 14=6, 16=6, 18=7, 23=4, 26=4, 30=5, 36=5, 40=5, 42=5

Factor II Resistance Against Anti-African Forces

Items: 3,8,9,13,15,17,31,32,33,37,41 (11 items)
Total Score: 52/88
Low Range

3=4, 8=8, 9=4, 13=5, 15=7, 17=4, 31=7, 32=4, 33=5, 37=4, 41=5

Factor III Value for African-Centered Institutions and Cultural Expressions

Items: 20,22,24,25,27,29,34,39 (8 items)
Total Score: 40/64
Low Range

20=5, 22=7, 24=7, 25=4, 27=6, 29=4, 34=5, 39=2

Factor IV Value for African Institutions and
Cultural Expressions

Items: 5,7,19,21,28 (5 items)
Total Score: 34/40
High Range

5=7, 7=8, 19=5, 21=8, 28=6

Total Score ASCS: 199/336
Middle Range Score on ASCS 127/251

#22
Factor I Collective African Identity and Self-Fortification

Items: 1,2,4,6,10,12,14,16,18,23,26,30,36,40,42 (15 items)
Total Score: 81/120
High Range

1=7, 2=7, 4=4, 6=7, 10=7, 12=7, 14=7, 16=6, 18=7, 23=2, 26=8, 36=7, 40=1, 42=1

Factor II Resistance Against Anti-African Forces

Items: 3,8,9,13,15,17,31,32,33,37,41 (11 items)
Total Score: 68/88
High Range

3=7, 8=6, 9=7, 13=5, 15=5, 17=7, 31=7, 32=3, 33=7, 37=6, 41=8

Factor III Value African-Centered Institutions and
Cultural Expressions

Items: 20,22,24,25,27,29,34,39 (8 items)
Total Score: 47/64
High Range

20=7, 22=7, 24=6, 25=2, 27=2, 29=8, 34=7, 39=8

Factor IV Value for African-Centered Institutions and Cultural Expressions

Items: 5,7,19,21,28 (5 items)
Total Score: 28/40
High Range: 20.5/40
Middle Range ASCS: 127/251
Range: 224/336

5=7, 7=2, 19=7, 21=4, 28=8

#23

Factor I Collective African Identity and Self-Fortification

Items: 1,2,4,6,109,12,16,18,23,26,30,36,40,42 (15 items)
Total Score: 96/120
High Range: 75.5/120

1=7, 2=8, 4=2, 6=6, 10=8, 12=6, 14=8, 16=8, 23=6, 26=7, 30=7, 36=8, 40=7, 42=6

Factor II Resistance Against Anti-African Forces

Items: 3,8,9,13,15,17,31,32,33,37,41 (11 items)
Total Score: 75/88
High Range: 55.5/88

3=8, 8=7, 9=7, 13=8, 15=7, 17=7, 31=7, 32=6, 33=3, 37=8, 41=7

Factor III Value for African-Centered Institutions and Cultural Expression

Items: 20,22,24,25,27,29,34,39 (8 items)
Total Score: 44/64
High Range: 40.5/64

20=8, 22=8, 24=5, 25=5, 27=3, 29=8. 34=4, 39=3

Factor IV Value for African-Centered Institution and Cultural Expression

Items: 5,7,19,21,28 (5 items)
Total Score: 30/40
High Range: 20.5/40

5=8, 7=6, 19=7, 21=7, 28=2

Total Score ASCS: 245/336
Middle Range ASCS 127/251

#24
Factor I Collective Identity and Self-Fortification

Items: 1,2,4,6,10,12,14,16,18,23,26,30,36,40,42 (15 items)
Total Score: 95/120
High Range: 75.5/120

1=6, 2=8, 4=4, 6=7, 10=8, 12=7, 14=7, 16=8, 18=2, 23=8, 26=7, 30=3, 36=5, 40=7, 42=8

Factor II Resistance Against Anti-African

Items: 3,8,9,13,15,17,31,32,33,37,41 (11 items)
Total Score: 6888
High Range: 55.5/88

3=4, 8=3, 9=7, 13=8, 15=7, 17=7, 31=8, 32=2, 33=8, 37=7, 41=7

Factor III Value for African-Centered Institutions and Cultural Expression

Items: 20,22,24,25,27,29.34.39
Total Score 44/64
High Range 40.5/64

20=7, 22=8. 24=7, 25=7, 27=2, 29=7, 34=6, 39=2

Factor IV Value for African-Centered Institution and Cultural Expression

Items: 5,7,19,21,28 (5 items)
Total Score: 30/40
High Range: 20/5/40

5=7, 7=1, 21=7, 28=4

Total Score ASCS: 245/336
Middle Range ASCA: 127/251

#25

Factor I Collective Identity and Self-Fortification

Items: 1,2,4,6,10,10,12,14,16,18,23,26,30,36,40,42 (15 items)
Total Score: 95/120
High Range: 75.5/120

1=2, 2=5, 4=4, 6=5, 10=8, 12=614=8, 16=6, 18=3, 23=8, 26=8, 30=8. 48. 41=8

Factor II Resistance Against Anti-African Forces

Items: 3,8,9,13,15,17,31,32,33,37,41 (11 items)
Total Score: 68/88
High Range: 55.5/88

3=5, 8=6, 9=5, 13=8, 15=4, 17=2.31=8, 32=8. 33=7, 37=7, 41=8

Factor III Value for African-Centered Institutions and Cultural Expression

Items: 20,22,24,25,27.29,24,39 (8 items)
Total Score 46/64
High Range: 40.5/64

20=7, 22=7, 24=8, 25=6, 27=7, 29=8, 34=8, 39=7

Factor IV Value for African-Centered Institution and Cultural Expression

Items: 5,7,19,21,28 (5 items)
Total Score: 27/40
High Range: 20.5/40

5=7, 7=7, 19=7, 21=8, 28=7

Total Score ASCA: 236/336
Middle Range ASCS: 127/251

#25

Factor I Collective African Identity and Self-Fortification

Items: 1,2,4,6,10,12,14,16,18,23,26,30,36,40,42 (15 items)
Total Score: 95/120
High Range: 75.5/120

1=2, 2=5, 4=4, 6=5, 10=8, 12=6, 14=8, 16=6, 18=3, 23=8. 26=8, 30=8, 36=8, 40=8, 42=8

Factor II Resistance Against Anti-African Forces

Items: 3,8,9,13,15,17,31,32,33,37,41 (11 items)
Total Score: 68/88
High Range: 55.5/88

3=5, 8=6, 9=5, 13=8, 15=4, 17=2, 31=8, 32=8, 33=7, 37=7, 41=8

Factor III Value for African-Centered Institutions and Cultural Expression

Items: 20,22,24,25,27,29,34,39 (8 items)
Total Score: 58/64
High Range: 40.5/64

20=7, 22=7, 24=8, 25=6, 27=7. 29=8, 34=8, 39=7

Factor IV Value for African-Centered Institution and Cultural Expression

Items: 5,7,19,21,28 (5 items)
Total Score: 36/40
High Range: 20.5/40

5==7, 7=7, 19=7, 21=8, 28=7

Total Score ASCS: 40/336
High Range: 257/336

#26

Factor I Collective African-Identity and Self-Fortification

Items: 1,2,4,6,10,12,14,16,18,23,26,30,36,40,42 (15 items)
Total Score: 112/120
High Range: 75.5/120

1=8, 2=8, 4=7, 6=8, 10=8, 12=1, 14=8. 16=8, 18=8, 23=8, 26=8, 30=8, 36= 8, 40=8, 42=8

Factor II Resistance Against Anti-African Forces

Items: 3,8,9,13,15,17,31,32,33,37,41
Total Score: 85/88
High Range: 55.5/88

3=8, 8=8, 9=8, 13=8, 15=8, 17=7, 31=8, 32=7, 33=8, 37=7, 41=8

Factor III Value for African-Centered Institutions and Cultural Expression

Items: 20,22,24,25,27,29,34,39
Total Score: 63/64
High Range: 40.5/64

20=8, 22=8, 24=8. 25=8, 27=8, 29=8, 34=7, 39=8

Factor IV Value African-Centered Institution and
Cultural Expression

Items: 5,7,19,21,28 (5 items)
Total Score: 39/40
High Range: 20.5/40

5=8, 7=8, 19=8, 21=8, 28=7

Total Score ASCS: 42/336
High Range ASCS: 299/336
252/336

#27

Factor I Collective African Identity and Self-Fortification

Items: 1,2,4,6,10,12,14,16,18,23,26,30,40,42 (15 items)
Total Score: 100/120
High Range: 75.5/120

1=5, 2=8, 4=7, 6-6, 10=8, 12=6, 14=6, 16=8, 18=1, 23=7, 26=7, 30=8, 36=8, 40=7, 42=8

Factor II Resistance Against Anti-African Forces

Items: 3,8,9,13,15,17,31,32,33,37 (11 items)
Total Score: 56/88
High Range: 55.5/88

3=7, 8=8, 9=7, 13-8, 15=8, 17=1, 32=5, 33=6, 37=1, 41=4

Factor III Value for African-Centered Institutions and
Cultural Expression

Items: 20,22,24,25,27,29,34,39 (8 items)
Total Score: 42/64
High Range: 40.5/64

20-7, 22=8, 24=5, 25=7, 27=1, 29=7, 34=3, 39=4

Factor IV Value for African-Centered Institution and Cultural Expression

Items: 5,7,19,21,28 (5 items)
Total Score: 33/40
High Range: 20.5/40

5=8, 7=6, 19=7, 21=7, 28=5

Total ASCS Range: 231/336
Middle Range ASCS: 127/251

#28

Factor I Collective African-Identity and Self-Fortification

Items: 1,2,4,6,10,12,14,16,18,23,26,30,36,40,42 (15 items)
Total Score: 94/120
High Range: 75.5/120

1=6, 2=8, 4=2, 6=4, 10=8, 12=8, 14=7, 16=6, 18=7, 23=8, 26=7, 30=3, 36=6, 40=6, 42=8

Factor II Resistance Against Anti-African Forces

Items: 3,8,9,13,15,17,31,32,33,37,41
Total Score: 79/88
High Range: 55.5/88

3=7, 8=7, 9=7, 13=8, 15=8, 17=8, 31=8, 32=2, 33=8, 37=8, 41=8

Factor III Value for African-Centered Institutions and Cultural Expression

Items: 20,22,24,25,27,29,34 (8 items)
Total Score: 39/64
Low Range: 8/40

20=2, 22=1, 24=6, 25=6, 27=5, 29=7, 34=8, 39=4

Factor IV Value for African-Centered Institution and Cultural Expression

Items: 5,7,19,21,28 (5 items)
Total Score: 34/40
High Range: 20.5/40

5=8, 7=8, 19=8, 21=8, 28=2

#29

Factor I Collective African Identity and Self-Fortification

Items: 1,2,4,6,10,12,14,16,18,23,30,36,40,42 (15 items)
Total Score: 90/120
High Range: 75.5/120

1=6, 2=8, 4=4, 6=3, 10=8, 12=6, 14=7, 16=8, 18=6, 23=8. 26=7, 30=5, 36=3, 40=6, 42=5

Factor II Resistance Against Anti-African Forces

Items: 3,8,9,13,15,17,31,32,33,37,41 (11 items)
Total Score: 65/88
High Range: 55.5/88

3=8, 8=6, 9=8, 13=7, 15=8, 17=4, 31=7, 32=7, 33=6, 37=3, 41=1

Factor III Value for African-Centered Institutions and Cultural Expression

Items: 20,22,24,25,27,29,34,39
Total Score: 43/64
High Range: 40.5/64

20=8, 22=8, 24=4, 25=7, 27=7, 29=8, 34=5, 39=1

Factor IV Value for African-Centered Institution and Cultural Expression

Items: 5,7,19,21,28 (5 items)
Total Score: 32/40

High Range: 20.5/40

5=7, 7=7, 19=7, 21=8, 28=3

Total Score ASCS: 42/336
Middle Range ASCS: 127/251

#30
Factor I Collective African Identity and Self-Fortification

Items: 1,2,4,6,10,12,14,16,18,23,26,30,36,40,42
Total Score: 87/120
High Range: 75.5/120

1=1, 2=5, 4=1, 6=5, 10=8. 12=8. 14=1, 16=8. 18=8, 23=8, 26=8, 30=3, 36=7, 40=8, 42=8

Factor II Resistance Against Anti-African Forces

Items: 3,8,9,13,15,17,31,32,33,37,41
Total Score: 78/88
High Range: 55.5/88

3=5, 8=8, 9=8, 13=8, 15=8, 17=8, 31=8, 32=7, 22=1, 37=8, 41=8

Factor III Value for African-Centered Institutions and Cultural Expressions

Items: 20,22,24,25,27,29 (8 items)
Total Score: 45/64
High Range: 40.5/64

20-8, 22=8, 24=8, 25=2, 27=2, 29=7, 34=7, 39=3

Factor IV Value for African-Centered Institution and Cultural Expression

Items: 5,7,19,21,28 (5 items)
Total Score: 32/30

5=6, 7=8, 19=8. 21=8, 28=2

Total Score ASCS: 42/336
Middle Range ASCS: 127/252
242/336

#31
Factor I Collective African Identity and Self-Fortification

Items: 1,2,4,6,10,12,14,16,18,23,26,30,36,40,42 (15 items)
Total Score: 83/120
High Range: 75.5/120

1=6, 2=5, 4=3, 6=8, 10=1, 12=7, 14=6, 16=7, 18=6, 23=8, 26=7, 30=4, 36=5, 40=5, 41=5

Factor II Resistance Against Anti-African Forces

Items: 3,8,9,13,15,17,31,32,33,37,41 (11 items)
Total Score: 60/88
High Range

3=5, 8=6, 9=6, 13=8, 15=7, 17=6, 31=7, 32=4

Factor III Value for African-Centered Institutions and Cultural Expression

Items: 20,22,24,25,27,29,34,39 (8 items)
Total Score: 42/64
High Range

20-6, 22=7, 24=8, 25=7, 27=3, 29=6, 34=3, 39=2

Factor IV Value for African-Centered Institution and Cultural Expression

Items: 5,7,19,21,28 (5 items)
Total Score: 34/40
High Range

1=7, 2=8, 4=8, 6=8, 10=8, 12=8, 14=8, 16=8, 18=7, 23=8, 26=8, 30=4, 36=8, 40=8, 42=8

Total ASCS Score: 219/336
Middle Range: 127/251

#32

Factor I Collective African Identity and Self-Fortification

Items: 1,2,4,6,10,12,14,16,18,23,26,30,36,40,42
Total Score: 109/120
High Range

1=7, 2=8, 4=8, 6=8, 10=8,.12=8, 14=8, 16=8. 18=7, 13=8, 26=8, 30=4, 36=8, 40=8, 41-8

Factor II Resistance Against Anti-African Forces

Items: 3,8,9,13,15,17,31,32,33,37,41, (11 items)
Total Score: 80/88
High Range: 55.5/88

3=6, 8=7, 9=8, 13=8, 15=7, 17=4, 31=8, 32=8, 33=8, 37=8, 4=8

Factor III Value for African-Centered Institution and Cultural Expression

Items: 20,22,24,25,27,29,34,39 (8 items)
Total Score: 46/64
High Range: 40.5/64

20=1, 22=8, 24=8, 25=8, 27=1, 29=8, 34=4, 39=8

Factor IV Value for African-Centered Institution and Cultural Expression

Items: 5,7,19,21,28 (5 items)
Total Score: 35/40
High Range

5==8, 7=8, 19=8, 21=8, 28=3

Total Score ASCS: 270/336

#33

Factor I Collective African Identity and Self-Fortification

Items: 1,2,4,6,10,12,14,16,23,26,30,40,42
Total Score: 69
High Range: 75.5/120
Low Range: 15/75

1=8, 2=5, 4=1, 6=6, 10=8, 12=5, 14=2, 16=4, 18=2, 23=8, 26=1, 30=8, 36=4, 40=1, 42=6

Factor II Resistance Against Anti-African Forces

Items: 3,8,9,13,15,17,31,32,33
Total Score: 82
High Range: 55.5/88
Low Range: 11/75

3=8, 8=8, 9=8, 13=8, 15=5, 17=8, 31=8, 32=8, 33=8, 37=8, 41=5

Factor III Value for African-Centered Institutions and Cultural Expressions

Items: 20,22,24,25,27,29,34,39
Total Score: 44
High Range: 40/5/64
Low Range: 8/40

20=8, 22=5, 24=3, 25=8, 27=8, 29=8, 34=3, 39=1

Factor IV Value for African-Centered Institution and Cultural Expression

Items: 5,7,19,21,28 (5 items)
Total Score: 30
High Range: 20.5/40
Low Range: 5/20

5=8, 7=5, 19=8, 21=8, 28=1

Total Score ASCS: 42/336
Middle Range: 225/232

#34

Factor I Collective African Identity and Self-Fortification

Items: 1,2,4,6,10,12,14,16,18,23,26,30,40,42
Total Score: 107
High Range: 75.5/120
Low Range: 15/75

1=8, 2=8, 4=2, 6=8,10=8, 12=8, 14=8, 16=8, 18=8, 23=8, 26=8, 30=8, 36=1, 40-8, 42=8

Factor II Resistance Against Anti-African Forces

Items: 3,8,9,13,15,17,31,32,33,37,41
Total Score: 88
High Range: 55.5/88
Low Range: 11/55

3=8, 8=8, 9=8, 13=8m 15=8, 17=8, 31-8,32=8, 33=8, 37=8, 41=8

Factor III Value for African-Centered Institutions and Cultural Expressions

Items: 20,22,24,25,27,28,34,39, (8 items)
Total Score: 63
High Range: 40.5/64
Low Range: 8/40

20=8, 22=8, 24=8, 25=8, 27=8, 29=8, 34=8, 39=7

Factor IV Value for African-Centered Institution and Cultural Expression

Items: 5,7,19,21,28 (5 items)
Total Score: 37
High Range: 20.5/40
Low Range: 5/20

5=8, 7=8, 19=8, 21=8, 28=5

Total ASCS Range: 40/336

Extra 3 = 11. 1=8. 35-5 38-8
Total 17
Total Score: 295 Extra 3 = 17
High Range: 252/336
Middle Score: 127/251
Low ASCS: 42/126

#35
Factor I Collective African Identity and Self-Fortification

Items: 1,2,4,6,10,12,14,16,18,23,26,30,36,40,42 (15 items)
Total Score: 108
High Range 255/120
Low Range: 15/75

1=8, 2=1, 48, 6=7, 10=8, 12=8, 14=8, 16=8, 18=7, 23=8, 26=8, 30=5, 36=8, 40=8, 42=8

Factor II Resistance Against Anti-African Forces

Items: 3,8,9,13,15,17,31,32,33,37,41 (11 items)
Total Score: 77
High Range: 55.5
Low Range: 11/55

3=8, 8=1, 9=8, 13=8, 15=8, 17=8, 31=8, 32=4, 33=8, 37=8, 41=8

Factor III Value for African-Centered Institutions and Cultural Expression

Item: 20,22,24,25,27,29,34 (8 items)
Total : 54
High Range: 40.5/64
Low Range: 8-40

20=8, 22=8, 24=6, 25=8, 27=8, 29=8, 34=7, 39=1

Factor IV Value for African-Centered Institution and Cultural Expression

Items: 5,7,19,21,28
Total: 39/40

5=8, 7=8, 19=8, 21=8, 28=7, 36=5, 40=5, 42=5

Total ASCS: Extra 3, 11.1=8 35.4=5. 38 – 1, Extra 14
ASCS – 292
High ASCS – 252/336
Middle ASCS – 127/251
Low ASCS – 42/126

#36

Factor I Collective African Identity and Self-Fortification

Items: 1,2,4,6,10,12,14,16,18,23,26,30,36,40,42
Total Score: 79/120
High Range: 75.5/120
Low Range: 15/75

1=1, 2=8, 4=4, 6=3, 10=7,12=6,14=8, 16=8, 18=2, 23=8, 26=8, 30=1, 36=6, 40=6, 42=8

Factor II Resistance to Anti-African Forces

Items: 3,8,9,13,15,17,31,32,33,37,41 (11 items)
Total: 67
High Range: 55.5/88
Low Range: 11/55
High Range: 67

3=2, 8=7,9=7,13=8,15=6,17=7,31=7,32=1,33=6=37=8,41=8

Factor III Value for African-Centered Institution and Culture Expression

Items: 20,22,24,25,27,2934,39
Total: 49
High Range: 40.5/64

Low Range: 8/40
20-8,22=8,24=8,25=7,27=7,29=6,34=2,39=3

Factor IV Value for African-Centered Institution and
Cultural Expression

Items: 5,7,19,21,28 (5 items)
Total: 28/40
High Range: 20.5/40
Low Range: 5-10

5=7, 7=2, 19=8,21=8,28=3

Total Extra: 3, 11 4=5, 35 3=6   38: 3
Extra Plus 14
Total ASCS – 223
237 – Middle ASCS

Total ASCS Score
High Score – 252/336
Middle Score = 127/251
Low ASCS

#37
Factor I Collective African Identity and Self-Fortification

Items: 1,2,4,6,10,12,14,16,18,23,26,30,36,40,42
Total Score : 94
High Range: 75.5/120
Low Range : 15/75
High Range: 94

1=3, 2=8,4=8,6=6,10=8,12=5,14=6,16=18=4,23=8,26=7,30=4,40=7,42-8

Factor II Resistance Against Anti-African Forces

Items: 3,8,9,13,15,17,31,32,33,37,41 (11 items)
Total Score: 74
High Range: 55.5/88
Low Range: 11/55

3-8,8-4,9-8,15-8,17-18-31-7,32-1,33-1=8,37-7,41=7

Factor III Value for African-Centered Institution and Cultural Expressions

Items: 20,22,24,25,27,29,34,39 (8 items)
Total Score: 56
High Range: 40.5/64
Low Range: 8/40

20=7,22=8,24=8,25=8,27=6,29=8,34=4,39=7

Factor IV Value for African-Centered Institution and Cultural Expression

Items: 5,7,19,21,28 (5 items)
Total Score: 30/40
High Range: 20.5/40
Low Range: 5/20

5=1,7=7,19=8,21=6,28=8

ASCS: 16 pts +254=270
High ASCS Score: 252-336
Middle ASCS Score: 127-251
Low ASCS Score: 42-126
High ASCS Score: 270

#38
Factor I Collective African Identity and Self-Fortification

Items: 1,2,4,6,10,12,14,16,18,23,26,30,36,40,42
Total Score: 80/120
High Range: 75.5/120
Low Range: 15/75
High Range: 80

1=4, 2-5,4=5,6=5,10=5,12=5,14=5,16=8,18=8,23=4,26=5,30=8,36=3,40=5,42=5

Factor II Resistance Against Anti-African Forces

Items: 3,8,9,13,15,17,31,32,33 (11 items)
Total Score: 41
High Range: 55.5/88

Low Range: 11/55
Low Range: 41

3=4,8=5, 9=4,13=1, 15=4, 17=5,31=5,32=4,33=4,37=4,41=1

Factor III Value for African-Centered Institution and Cultural Expressions

Items: 20,22,24,25,27,29,34,39 (8 items)
Total Score: 34
High Range: 40.5/64
Low Range: 8/40
Low Range: 34

20=5,22=5,24=5,25=4,27=4,29=1,34=5,39=5

Factor IV Value for African-Centered Institution and Cultural Expression

Items: 5,7,19,21,28 (5 items)
Total Score: 20
High Range: 20.5/40
Low Range: 5/20
Low Range: 20

5=4,7=4,19=4,21,21,28=4

Total ASCS Score
Extra: 11- 5=4, 35- 5=4. 38- 1
Total ASCS=9 + 175=184
Middle Score: 184
High ASCS: 252/336
Middle ASCS: 127/251
Low ASCS: 42/126

#39

Factor I Collective African Identity and Self-Fortification

Items: 1,2,4,6,10,12,14,16,18,23,26,30,36,40,42
Total Score: 110

High Range: 75.5/120
Low Range: 15/75
High Range: 110

1=8,2=8,4=5,6=6,10=8,12=5,14=8,16=8,18=8,23=8,26=8,30=6,40=8,42=8

Factor II Resistance Against Anti-African Forces

Items: 3,8,9,13,15,17,31,32,33
Total Score: 75
High Range: 55.5/88
Low Range: 11/55
High Range : 75

3=5,8=8,9=8,13=8,15=8,17=5,31=8,32=8,33=8,37=1,41=8

Factor III Value for African-Centered Institutions and Cultural Expressions

Items: 20,22,24,25,27,29,34,39 (8 items)
Total Score: 58
High Range: 40.5/88
Low Range: 8/40

20=8,22=8,24=5,25=8,27=7,29=8,34=6,39=8

Factor IV Value for African-Centered Institution and Cultural Expression

Items: 5,7,19,21,28 (5 items)
Total Score: 35
High Range: 20.5/40
Low Range: 5/20

5=8,7=8,19=5,21=8,28=6,42=5

Total ASCS: 11. – 1. 35-4.38-4
Total 9pts + 278 = 287
Total ASCS: 287
High Score: 252/336
Middle Range: 127/251

Low Range: 42/126
HighRange: 287

#40
Factor I Collective African Identity and Self-Fortification

Items: 1,2,4,6,10,12,14,16,18,23,26,30,36,40,42 (15 items)
Total Score: 105
High Range: 75.5/120
Low Range: 15/75
High Range: 105

1=7,2=8,4=5,6=7,10=8,12=7,14=8,16=7,18=7,23=2,26=8,30=8,36=8,40=7,42=8

Factor II Resistance to Anti-African Forces

Items: 3,8,9,13,15,17,31,32,33,37,41
Total Score: 72
High Range: 55.5/88
Low Range: 11/15
High Range: 72

3=5,8=2,9=8,13=8,15=2,17=7,31=8,32=8,33=8,37=8,41=8

Factor III Value for African-Centered Institutions and Cultural Expressions

Items: 20,22,24,25,27,29,34,39
Total Score: 53
High Range: 40.5/64
Low Range: 8/40
High Range: 53

20=8,22=8,24=8,25=7,27=8,29=5,34=7,39=2

Factor IV Value for African Culture

Items: 5,7,19,21,28 (5 items)
Total Score: 25
High Range: 20.5/40

Low Range: 5/20
High Range: 25

5=7,7=2,19=7,21=2,28=7

Total ASCS: 11-3, 35-8, 38-8
19 pts Extra
19+ 255= 274 High Range
High Range: 252/336
Middle Range: 127/251
Low Range: 42/126

Observation: Naming Ceremony
Sample of Field Notes

Event Observed: Naming Ceremony
Place: Shrine of the Black Madonna
Time: 2:00 p.m. Saturday
May 5, 2011
Ceremony Held at History Class. Led by MWalimu Oluntunji.
The person was introduced as a neophyte preparing to receive his African name. He was
given several books including *Black Messiah* and *Black Christian Nationalism* by Rev.
Cleage. When we met two weeks later, the MWalimu announced the person had passed
the Initial Stage. He was handed his name and its memory. He was called by his new
name, symbolizing his role as a warrior.

Response
The people were happy to see someone trying to leave the slave name that we carry. He
was welcomed as a new warrior for liberation of Black people. We talked about how we
must build the new nation. A black nation and our relationship with Israel and Jah.

Sample of Field Notes

Event Observed: Worship Service
Place: Shrine of the Black Madonna Sanctuary
Time: 10:00 Am - End 2:00pm
Participate, service, Sermon by Cardinal MWende Brown
Sermon, prayer, prepare and proceed
People responded with "Amen, Can I get a witness?"
Music performed by the band, singing, and communion. Singing of the Black National
Anthem

Response
The people were very enthusiastic about the message. The people sang to the music and
were clapping and witnessing as observed. I found the service to be spiritually satisfying.
I participated in the services and understood that what we call church is our
acknowledgment of the Spirit of God within us.

Sample Field Notes

Observation: History Class
Event Observed: History Class
Place: Shrine of the Black Madonna

Date: December 8, 2012
Time: 1:50pm – End 3:30pm
Class attended - participants
Session led by MWamuli Oluntunji
Topics discussed:
      Ghana
      Mali
      Songhay
Students responded by asking questions regarding the lesson and videos shown.

Response

I found students to be very active and very inquisitive about the discussions. Students read out loud and handouts were distributed during the lessons as observed. I found the session to be stimulating and it created a sense of pride in the people. Everyone enjoyed the video of Mali Sankore University in Timbuctu.

Observation: Naming Ceremony
Sample of Field Notes

Event Observed	Response
Event Observed: Naming Ceremony Place: Shrine of the Black Madonna Time: 2:00 p.m. Saturday May 5, 2011 Ceremony held at History Class. Led by MWalimu Oluntunji. The person was introduced as a neophyte preparing to receive his African name. He was given several books- Black Messiah and Black Christian Nationalism by Rev. Cleage. When we met two weeks later the MWalimu announced the person had passed the Initial Stage. He was handed his name and its memory. He was called by his new name, symbolizing his role as a warrior.	The people were happy to see someone trying to leave the slave name that we carry. He was welcomed as a new warrior for the liberation of black people. We talked about how we must build the new nation. A Black Nation and our relationship with Israel and Jah.

Obesrvation: Worship Service
Sample of Field Notes

Event Observed	Response
Event Observed: Worship Service Place: Shrine of the Black Madonna Sanctuary Time: 10:00 Am - End 2:00pm Participate, service, Sermon by Cardinal MWende Brown Sermon, prayer, prepare, and proceed. People responded with "Amen, Can I get a witness?" Music by the band, singing, and communion. Singing of the Black National Anthem	The people were very enthusiastic about the message. The people sang to the music and were clapping and witnessing as observed. I found the service to spiritually satisfying. I participated in the services and understood that what we call church is our acknowledgment of the Spirit of God within us.

History Class
Sample of Field Notes

Event Observed	Response
Observation: History Class Event Observed: History Class Place: Shrine of the Black Madonna Date: December 8, 2012 Time: 1:50 p.m. – End 3:30 p.m. Class attended - participants Session led by MWamuli Oluntunji Topics discussed: Ghana, Mali, and Songhay Students responded by asking questions regarding the lesson and videos shown.	I found students to be very active and very inquisitive about the discussions. Students read out loud and there are handouts during the lessons as observed. I found the session to be stimulating and it created a sense of pride in the people. Everyone emjoyed the video of Mali Sankore and the University in Timbuctu.

Baldwin, Joseph A. *The African Personality in America*. Tallahassee, FL: Nubian Nation Publications, 1993.

_____. *Afrocentric Cultural Consciousness and African American Afrocentric Visions*. London: Sage Publication, 1998.

Baldwin, Joseph A. "African Self Consciousness and the Mental Health of African Americans." *Journal of Black Studies 15*, No 2 (December 1984): 174-187

_____. "Notes on an Afrocentric Theory of Black Personality." *Journal of Black Psychology 5*, No. 2 (August 1987): 133-148.

Ben Jochannan, Yosef. *Cultural Genocide: In the Black and African Studies Curriculum*. Baltimore, MD: Black Classic Press, 1972.Blyden, Edward W. *Christianity Islam and the Negro Race*. Baltimore, MD: Black Classic Press (1888), 1994.

Bishop, AyannaAbi and Cardinal Ammifu Waganga.."The PAOCC Synod '96: A call to Revolutionary struggle," (June 17-20, 1996).

Bishop Oluufum, General Chairman Officator. The Shrine of the Black Madonna. National Pan African Synod (July 5-8, 1993).

Bretman, George. Ed. *Malcolm X By Any Means Necessary*. New York: Path Finder, 1970.

Carruthers, Jacob H. *Intellectual Warfare*. Chicago: Third World Press, 1999.

Clark, Cedric X et al. "Voodoo or I.Q: An Intro to African Psychology." *Journal of Black Psychology 1*, No. 2 (February 1975): 9-29.

Clark, John Henry. *Malcolm X: The Man and His Times*. Trenton, NJ: Africa World Press, 1990.

Cleage, Albert. *The Black Messiah*. Trenton, NJ: African World Press, 1989.

_____. *BCN: Black Christian Nationalism*. Detroit, MI: Luxor Publishers, 1972

Cone, James H. *A Black Theology of Liberation*. Maryknoll, NY: Orbis Books, 1984.

Conyers, James L. Jr. Ed. *African Studies: A Disciplinary Quest for both theory and Method*. London: McFarland and Company Inc., 1997.

Cresswell, John W. *Qualitative Inquiry and Research Design: Choosing among Five Approaches*, 3rd ed. (Los Angeles: Sage Publications), 2003.

Delaney, Martin R. *The Condition Elevation and Destiny of the Colored People in the United States*. Baltimore, MD: Black Classic Press, 1993.

Diop, Cheikh Anta. *Precolonial Black Africa*. New York: Lawrence Hill Books, 1987.

_____. *Toward the African Renaissance*. London: Kurnac House, 1996.

Ebulem, Nwaka Chris. *The Power of Africentric Celebration: The Inspiration from the Zairean Litergy*. New York: The Crossroad Publishing Co., 1996.

Fanon, Frantz. *Black Skin, White Mask*. New York: Grove Press, 1967.

_____. *The Wretched of the Earth*. New York: Grove Press, 1963.

Fundi, Natak Mosheshe. "BCN 1975 Biannual Convention of Black Christian Nationalism Church." Shrine of the Black Madonna (April 1-6, 1975).

Frazier, E. Franklin. *Black Bourgeoise*. New York: The Free Press, 1957.

Garvey, Amy Jacques. Ed. *The Philosophy and Opinions of Marcus Garvey*. Dover, MA: The Majority Press, 1986.

Hamlet, Janice D. Ed. *Afrocentric Visions*. Thousand Oaks, CA: Sage Publications, 1998).

James, George G. M. *Stolen Legacy*. Trenton, NJ: Africa World Press, 1954.

Joseph, P. E. "Black Liberation Without Apology: Reconceptualizing the Black Power Movement." *The Black Scholar 31*, No. 3-4 (Fall 2001 - Winter 2002): 2-19.

Kambon, K. K. *African/Black Psychology in the American Context: An African Centered Approach*. Tallahassee, FL: Nubian Nation Publications, 1998.

Karenga, Maulana. *MAAT: The Moral Ideal in Ancient Egypt*. Los Angeles: University of Sankore Press, 2006.

Kimati, Juramogi Memelik. "The Pan African Orthodox Christian Church," (2000).

Kwate, Naa Oyo A. "The Heresy of African Centered Psychology." *Journal of Medical Humanities 26*, No. 4 (Winter 2005): 215-235.

Kwate, Nga Oyo A. Cross. "Validation of the Afrocentric Scale." *Journal of Black Psychology 29* (August 2003): 308-14.

Latif, S. A., and Latif, N. *The African American Psychic Trauma.* Chicago: Latif Communications Group, Inc., 1994.

Lincoln, C. Eric. *The Black Muslims in America.* New York: Koyode Publications, Ltd., 1961.

Madhubuto, Hki R. *Black Men Obsolete, Single and Dangerous? The African American Family in Transition: Essays in Discovery, Solution and Hope.* Chicago: Third World Press, 1991.

Martin, Tony. *Race First: The Ideological and Organizational Struggle of Marcus Garvey and the Universal Negro Improvement Association.* Dover: The Majority Press, 1976.

Maxim, Paul S. *Quantitative Research Methods in the Social Sciences.* New York: Oxford University Press, 1990.

Mazama, Ama. *The Afrocentric Paradigm.* Trenton, NJ: African World Press, 2003

Myers, Linda J. *Understanding an Afroccentric Worldview.* Dubuque, IA: Kendall/Hunt Publication Co., 1998.

Nyrere, Sondai. First Cardinal Regional Bishop of the Southern Region Atlanta, GA. Shrine of the Black Madonna 10th anniversary of Shrine # 10 National Tribute to Jaramogi Abebe Agyeman," (June 1987).

Oshodi, John Egberazien. "Then Construction of an Afrocentric Sentence Completion Test to Assess the Need for Achievement." *Journal of Black Studies 30,* No. 2, (November 1999): 216-231.

Parham, Thomas A., White, Joseph L. and Adisa, Ajamu. *The Psychology of Blacks.* Upper Saddle River, NJ: Prentice Hall, Inc., 1984.

Schiele, Jerome H. "Organizational Theory from an Afrocentric Perspective." *Journal of Black Studies 21,* No. 2 (December 1990): 149-155.

Shrine of the Black Madonna. *National Recommitment Sunday Commemorative Booklet,* (June 14, 1888).

Shrine of the Black Madonna. Tenth Anniversary of Shrine #10, "National Tribute to Jaramogi Agyeman," (June 1987).

Sis.Andongwisue, Ishara Shrine of the Black Madonna. "Portriat of a Servant. The Life Views and Teachings of Our Founder and Holy Patriatch Jaramogi Abebe Agyeman," (June 14, 1998).

Starkey, Carolyn, Dara. "Jublee Souvenir Booklet," Shrine of the Black Madonna (August 1-3, 2003).

Thiong'o, Ngugi Wa. *Decolonizing the Mind: The Politics of Language in African Literature.* Chicago: Third World Press, 1993.

Walker, David. *David Walker's Appeal.* Baltimore, MD: Black Classic Press (1830), 1993.

Waters, Kenneth L. *Afrocentric Sermons: The Beauty of Blackness in the Bible.* Valley Forge, PA: Judson Press, 1993.

Wilson, Amos. *Black on Black Violence: The Psychodynamic of Black Self-Annihilation in Service of White Domination.* New York: African World Infosystems, 1990.

_____. *Blueprint for Black Power.* New York: African World Infosystems, 1998.

Wright, W.D. *Crisis of the Black Intellectual.* Chicago: The Third World Press, 17.

Yeshitchla, Omali. *The Dialectics of Black Revolution: The struggle to Defeat the Counter Insurgency in the U. S.* Oakland, CA: Burning Spear Uhuru Publications, 1997.

Printed in the United States
By Bookmasters